Cursive Writing

Made Easy & Fun!

101 Quick, Creative Activities & Reproducibles That Help Kids of All Learning Styles Master Cursive Writing

by Kama Einhorn

SCHOLASTIC
PROFESSIONAL BOOKS

New York • Toronto • London • Auckland • Sydney • Mexico City • New Delhi • Hong Kong

a b c d e f g h i j k l m n o p q r s t u v w x y z

For my parents, Martin Einhorn and Karen Macri Einhorn,
who nurtured my love of letters from the beginning.

Acknowledgments

Grateful thanks to Liza Charlesworth, Terry Cooper, and Janelle Cherrington for their thoughtful consideration and editorial insight. Special thanks to Samantha Berger for her endless support and rhyming genius, to Mark McVeigh for his valuable suggestions, to Jennifer Levin Boss for her teacher's logic, and to Matty White, for love and patience.

Edited by Janelle Cherrington

Cover design by Norma Ortiz

Cover illustration by Michael Moran

Interior design by Ellen Matlach Hassell
for Boultinghouse & Boultinghouse, Inc.

Interior Illustrations by Michael Moran and Manuel Rivera

ISBN 0-439-11369-5

Printed in the U.S.A.

a b c d e f g h i j k l m n o p q r s t u v w x y z

Contents

Introduction

Easing In

Letter Practice

a b c d e f g h i j k l m n o p q r s t u v w x y z

Introduction

We need letters. Somehow, these 26 abstract building blocks—each with its own unique arrangement of lines, curves, or dots—work together in endless combinations to represent ideas. We need to copy these forms clearly and consistently in order to record our thoughts on paper in a way that others can understand.

We all know the pride young students (and their teachers and family members!) take in their first attempts at writing these forms and in the important steps they take in kindergarten and first grade on the way to becoming writers. Children are highly motivated to learn to write.

But how do we keep that sense of wonder, that joy of getting "lost in the letters" alive as second and third graders take on the new challenge of writing in cursive? Nurturing a love of writing is one of the many things teachers already do; how can we integrate this new form of written communication into our work and create another strong, fun diving board from which children can jump into the exhilarating pool of literacy?

Welcome to Cursive Writing Made Easy & Fun!

Curvy letters, "script," fancy writing, grown-up letters—no matter what students call it, cursive is a writing system that requires practice to learn. Like all writing systems, it's full of random, abstract symbols requiring our attention.

Students can explore the beauty of our writing system and take pride in their written work when they are having fun learning and creating cursive letters. Coupled with their strong desire to learn to write like adults or older brothers and sisters, learning cursive is a motivational building block for students' future literacy development: when students enjoy putting pencil to paper, and see their writing as a form of individual expression, they are more likely to do more of it!

Cursive, Script, Print, Manuscript—What's the Difference?

Cursive comes from the Latin *currere,* which means "to run."

Script, as cursive is often called, comes from the Latin *scribere,* "to write," and can be used to describe any system of writing.

Print refers to the stick-and-ball formation of letters that students learn before cursive.

Manuscript is the technical name for print.

Throughout this book, mainly *cursive* and *script* will be used.

Why Teach Cursive?

As adults, it's easy to forget that the English-language writing system requires students to recognize and write *four different forms* (upper- and lowercase manuscript and upper- and lowercase cursive) of each letter! Learning cursive puts a new set of alphabet recognition and fine-motor demands on students. Yet most of us continue to teach it, for many good reasons:

Expectations in school. Many English speakers use cursive when they write, and students should be able to recognize this written form. Some fourth-grade teachers use only cursive on the board and may require students to write in cursive. "You need it for fourth grade!" is a common reason students give for learning cursive.

Quick word recognition. Adams (1990) notes that automatic, accurate, and fast recognition of written words frees up mental energy. When students do not struggle to decode words written in cursive, they can concentrate on higher-order thinking.

Speed and ease of word formation. Many people find it faster and more comfortable to write in cursive, because the letters are connected and there is a rhythm and flow to writing with them. Without the "jerky" movements of manuscript writing, students do not have to lift their pencil to form each part of each letter or the next letter. Cursive can be thought of as the glue that holds words together, allowing for a whole-word approach rather than the examination of single letters.

Personal expression. Writing is the product of an individual, and no two people write alike. As students develop writing skills and styles, handwriting becomes a form of personal expression—students enjoy developing their own signatures and "decorating" their penmanship (Ruddell 1995). Students need to learn the cursive system to develop their own personal, legible, and consistent handwriting style; they should have the opportunity to explore cursive to see if it is right for them. (Many adults use a combination of manuscript and cursive, even within the same word!)

Prestige. Many students view cursive as "grown-up" writing. They take pride, for example, in being able to write their name in cursive before it has been formally taught. They may see their older family members or siblings using this writing system and view the learning of cursive as a rite of passage, like the school milestone of using pen rather than pencil.

Decoding in the print-rich world. In an increasingly media-saturated society, students must be able to recognize a wide variety of typefaces and writing styles in their environment. Even students who write on a computer can choose from many different fonts and sizes to communicate different effects.

Fewer letter reversals. Since cursive uses a continuous line, and the letters look a little different, some of the letter reversals that occur in manuscript writing (*b* and *d, p,* and *q*) may be eliminated.

Using This Guide

Students learn letter formation best through active exploration of letter names, the sounds the letters stand for, each letter's visual characteristics, and the motor movements involved in their formation (Bear et al. 1996). In order to help you combine and apply all of these all of these approaches to teaching cursive, we've divided this book into the following sections:

Easing In Activities The activities in this section prepare students for cursive instruction. They are designed to familiarize students with the cursive alphabet and concepts before they begin explicit writing practice—and to stimulate their interest! Students notice, observe, and have fun with the new letters.

Letter Practice Since writing in cursive is essentially a technical skill, this section contains reproducibles for writing practice. Students practice individual letters, then words. Letters are grouped and presented as having a "personality" that students can recognize, because letters are learned through repeated exposure to predictable features (Kuhl and Dewitz 1994). In other words, letters are taught according to similarity of formation. In addition, each letter is introduced with an accompanying story or rhyming directions that guide its formation. Each page in this section can be reproduced as many times as needed. Cut-out letter cards in the back of the book supplement these pages and can also be used in many of the activities in the next section.

Activities for All Learning Modalities Because we know that all children *can* learn, but they do not all learn the same way, this section is intended to make learning effective and enjoyable for each child's different learning style. Rich activity banks with fun, engaging activities for visual, tactile, kinesthetic, and auditory learners are provided.

Profiles of each learning style focus on the strengths and challenges of different learners in terms of handwriting instruction. The Suggested Sequence chart on page

11 links activities with specific letters; activities are presented in order of difficulty. However, you can also pick and choose activities to meet each student's individual needs. You can integrate the activities to introduce a letter, inspire additional practice, or reinforce certain letters. Note that activities having the potential to be a little bit messy are indicated by this icon.

Handwriting Hospital provides students with fun ways to assess and improve their handwriting and gives you clear ways to guide their improvement. Students "diagnose" and "treat" sample handwriting according to the "five S's of cursive" (size, slant, spacing, smoothness, and shape) as well as their own. When students have mastered all the letters and fine-tuned their handwriting, it's time for a "Certificate of Handwriting Health"!

Did You Know...

In the nineteenth century, many adults went to penmanship school. Good penmanship was seen as a sign of intelligence and social status.

A Suggested Sequence

No matter how compressed or spread out your timetable for cursive instruction, you'll want to focus on letter groups by teaching several letters with similar formations at one time. This will help students see the similarities between the letters and organize their visual perceptions. Lowercase letters are taught before capitals since they are used more frequently when students write.

A relaxed timetable would introduce between three and seven new letters per week. Including a week of Easing In activities, this would equal roughly ten weeks of instruction. This would allow you to teach letters in groups according to how they're formed and allow students to experience the letters in an orderly, leisurely fashion. Depending on your assessment of students' progress and interest level, you might choose to adjust the pace.

You also needn't wait until all your students have mastered every letter before dipping into the activity section; rather, use the activity links on the Suggested Sequence grid on page 11 as you see fit. Take your cues from your observations of students' writing and progress.

A Suggested Sequence

Letters	Type of Letter	Week 1	2	3	4	5	6	7	8	9	10	Suggested Activity Links
Easing In	Introductory Activities	**I**	**I**									1, 2, 3, 4, 7, 8, 10
Lowercase Letters												
i t u w e l b	Mountain Climbers		**I**	**M**	**M**	**M**	**M**	**M**	**M**	**M**	**M**	5, 6, 9, 11, 12, 15, 24, 25, 26, 34, 44
h k r s f p j	Mountain Climbers			**I**	**M**	**M**	**M**	**M**	**M**	**M**	**M**	14, 15, 24, 26, 29, 31, 34, 35, 36, 38, 41, 42
a d g q o c	Downhill Daredevils				**I**	**M**	**M**	**M**	**M**	**M**	**M**	15, 16, 21, 24, 26, 28, 30, 31, 34, 35, 36, 38, 41, 42
n m v x y z	Lumpy Letters					**I**	**M**	**M**	**M**	**M**	**M**	13, 15, 17, 18, 19, 20, 21, 24, 26, 29, 31, 34, 35, 37, 38, 41, 44
Uppercase Letters												
A O D C E Q	Backward Balloons						**I**	**M**	**M**	**M**	**M**	15, 20, 24, 26, 31, 32, 43
I J N M W H K X	Lefties & Curly-Qs							**I**	**M**	**M**	**M**	15, 20, 24, 26, 31, 32, 43
U Y V Z	Curly-Qs								**I**	**M**	**M**	22, 24, 26, 31, 33
P R B T F	Kickstarts & Tabletops									**I**	**M**	24, 26, 31, 33, 40
G S L	Capital Mountain									**I**	**M**	23, 24, 44

I = introduce **M** = maintain

a b c d e f g h i j k l m n o p q r s t u v w x y z

Letter Groupings

Letters are grouped according to their beginning strokes and difficulty of formation. Letters are introduced in this order:

Lowercase

Mountain Climbers have uphill beginnings.

i t u w e l b h k r s f p j

Downhill Daredevils have downhill beginnings.

a d g q o c

Lumpy Letters have over-the-hill "lumps."

n m v x y z

Uppercase

Backward Balloons have round, right-to-left downhill beginnings.

A O D C E Q

Lefties start with a swing to the left.

I J

Curly Qs have "fancy" beginnings.

N M W H K X U Y V Z

Kickstarts are named for their little beginning stroke.

P R B

Tabletops have flat tops.

T F

Capital Mountains share the same formation as lowercase Mountain Climbers.

G S L

Cursive Across the Curriculum

Language arts and cursive are naturally integrated. By infusing cursive into your math and technology programs, you can begin communicating the message that cursive is important throughout the curriculum, in all kinds of writing, and that it can be part of all the work we do.

Math Help students invent a cursive number-letter code, for instance, $a = 1$, $b = 2$, and so on.

- Challenge students to decode a word "spelled" with numbers and write the word in cursive. For example:

  2, 15, 2, 2, 25 *spells Bobby.*

- Pose a problem, such as 4 × 2, 5 × 1, 4 × 3, 6 + 6, 20 – 5. Have students do the computations and figure out each result. Then translate the resultant numbers into letters. Ask: *Together, what do the results spell?* Tell students to write their answer in cursive. For example:

  8, 5, 12, 12, 15 *spells hello.*

Science Most students are asked to label diagrams and drawings as part of their science curriculum. Encourage children to do all of their labeling in cursive.

Technology Most students love to experiment with different fonts and point sizes when writing on the computer. You might also invite students to play with their writing using drawing or painting programs.

And all over the room . . .
Begin using cursive in small ways: write the date and homework assignments on the board, students' names on their cubbies, chart and graphs around the room, and on all labels and signs. In addition, you might use cursive as a reward; for instance, once a student learns to write his name in cursive, he may head his papers that way from then on.

Cursive Q & A

How do I assess students' writing?
Is it reasonable to grade handwriting?

Consistency and legibility should be the goal. Do you know many adults who normally write like the models that we provide for students? Of course not! While students learn the formation of letters from a "perfect" model, they will naturally develop their own style. It's fine if their writing seems to slant backward or stand straight up rather than forward. The key is consistency throughout.

Standards for letter formation should consider whether the letter can be distinguished clearly from other letters. Other considerations include consistent, standard letter size and spacing between letters, words, and sentences.

When you mark students' work, you might circle their handwriting as well as words or letters that are difficult to read, and you might also provide narrative feedback, such as *Great slant! Watch your spacing.* Handwriting Hospital provides a fun, student-centered system of assessment, with the bottom line being the ability to read students' writing with ease.

It will also be useful to refer to the "Five S's of Cursive":

- **Size:** Letters are the right height and rest neatly on the line.

size size

- **Slant:** Letters all slant in one consistent direction, usually forward or straight up. A backward slant is also fine.

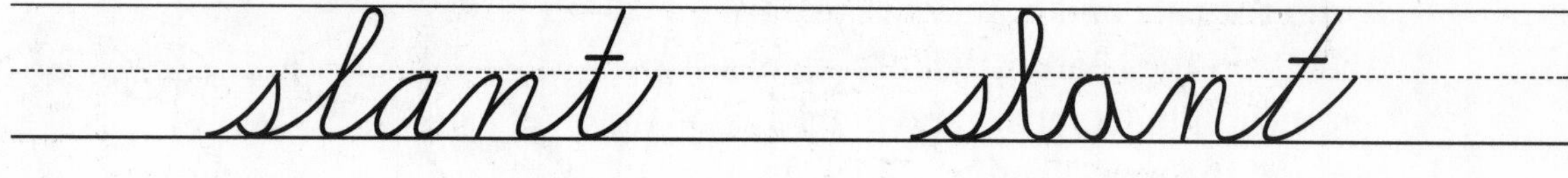

- **Shape:** Letters are closed where they should be; they are not too narrow or wide.

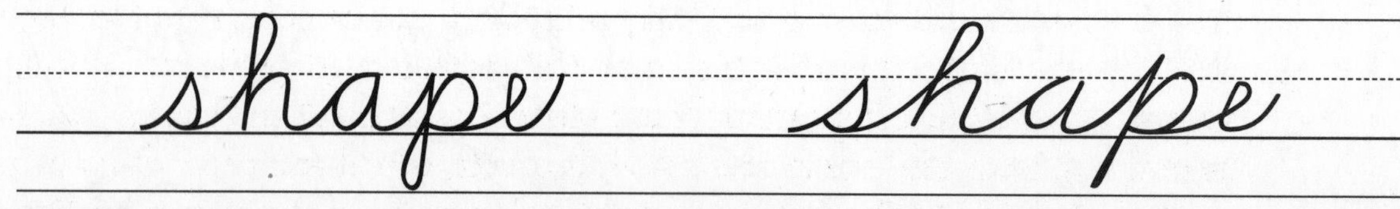

- **Spacing:** Spaces between letters, words, and sentences are even.

spacing spacing

- **Smoothness:** Line quality is even, not too light or heavy, or inconsistent.

smooth smooth

Do I need to adjust my teaching strategies for left-handed students?

Left-handed students may be unable to see the model at the beginning of a practice line because their hand is covering it up. The practice pages in this book include a model letter at the end of the line so that a model will always be visible. Also, left-handed students should slant their paper in the opposite direction of right-handed learners (see page 25). You might notice that these learners write with a backward slant; this is perfectly acceptable.

How can I help family members support students in this area?

Family members may be concerned with the "proper" way to write and may want to provide students with extra practice at home. They may be concerned that their child's handwriting is messy or that their child is frustrated by the new writing system. While explicit instruction of each letter has its place and letters need to be memorized, be careful not to prescribe lots of rote, pencil-and-paper at-home practice for students having difficulties. You might look over the student's handwriting sample with the family member and identify specific letters or joinings of letters that are presenting problems. Suggest to family members that they help students practice those problematic letters at home for five minutes a day. Stress for parents the importance of limiting practice time and providing students with a fun activity (for instance, practicing several rows of those particular letters and then decorating the sidewalk with any letters they want in chalk may be a good idea). This way, writing practice won't be viewed as a punishment or dreaded activity.

What challenges might second-language learners face?

Students unfamiliar with the English alphabet may still be busy learning the manuscript forms of each letter. Depending on the learner, you may decide to slow cursive instruction down a bit, or allow the student to work at her own pace. It will also help if you remember to review the meanings of English words and sentences before having ESL students write. Using visuals wherever possible is a great way to ensure that ESL students understand the words they are copying. The good news is that many students find cursive practice relaxing and fun. Furthermore, such concentrated attention on individual letters and words may prove worthwhile. Base your decision on time, other curriculum demands, and the student's frustration level.

Easing In Activities

The following activities will help students focus and prepare to learn cursive. Use them before you begin the letter practice on page 25.

Students are introduced to the idea of continuous-line writing by playing a high-interest game.

GROUP SIZE: WHOLE GROUP

MATERIALS a piece of string tied in a large loop

FIRST, many students enjoy string games. Ask volunteers to come to the front of the room and demonstrate the formations they can create with the string.

NEXT, as students observe, ask the group: *Why are we observing this game as we prepare to learn cursive?* Bring out the idea that cursive uses one continuous line to form words, and that careful steps taken in the right order form correct letters—just like string games form certain shapes.

LAST, challenge students to try to create the same shapes using different steps. Discuss their results.

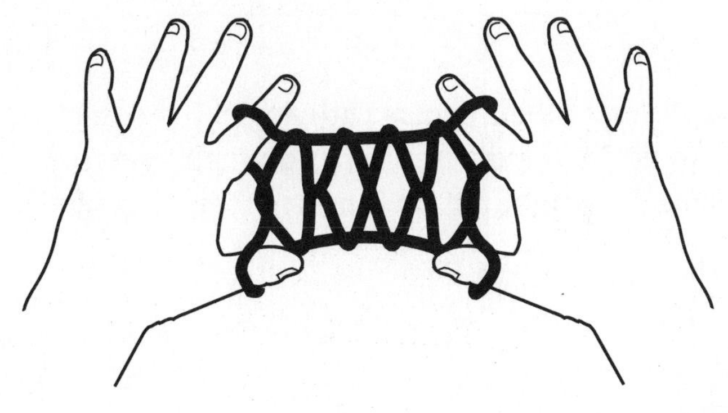

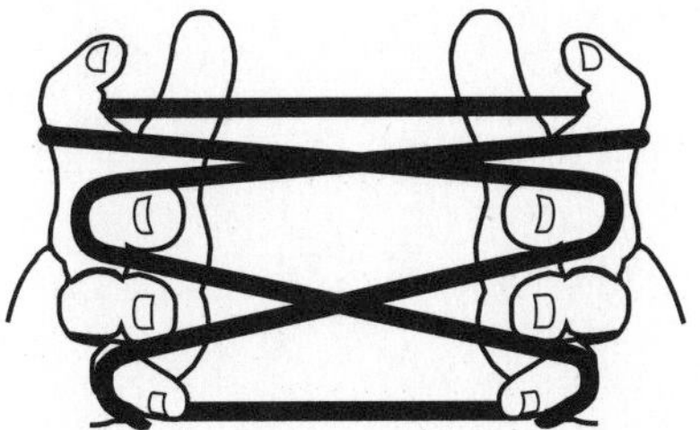

2 Continuous-Line Doodles

Students are introduced to the concept of unbroken lines by playing with decorative lines and exercising fine motor skills.

GROUP SIZE: INDIVIDUALS

MATERIALS lined paper, felt-tip markers in different colors, pencils

FIRST, draw these simple line doodles on the board and explain to students that cursive uses unbroken lines to create words. State: *This is a way to "warm up" our hands and fingers.*

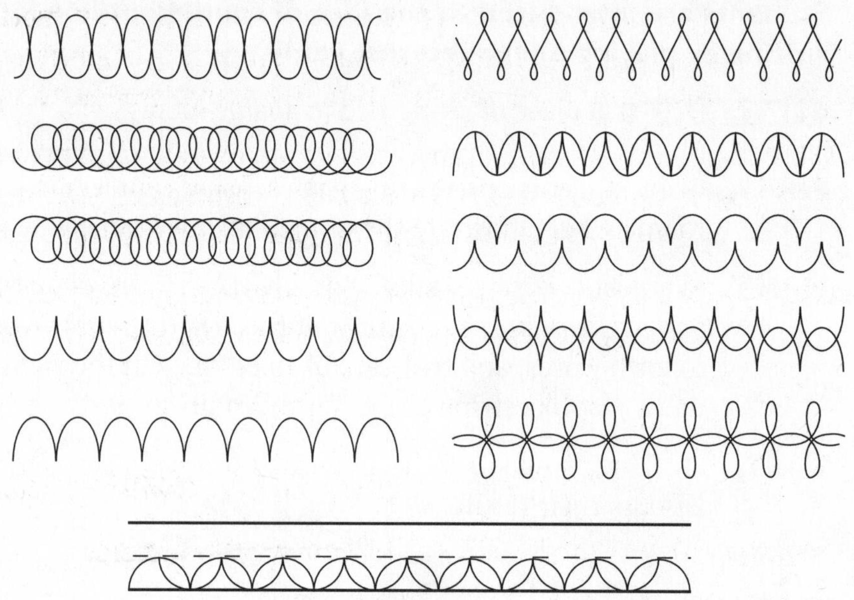

NEXT, invite students to decorate their papers with any of the designs in any colors. Encourage them to notice the different lines on their papers and write within any lines they want. You might put on music for this activity.

LAST, display their work.

3 Sign Up!

Students explore signatures and try to recognize most cursive letters.

GROUP SIZE: INDIVIDUALS

MATERIALS one copy of page 84 for each student, pencils, butcher paper

FIRST, as a group, discuss various uses of signatures: for legal agreements, signing checks and letters, receiving packages, and so on. Invite students to examine the signatures of famous people on the top half of the page and connect them to their manuscript versions. You might discuss with students the different "messages" that the signatures communicate. Ask students: *Is the signer fast? Orderly? Does the signer like to "decorate"? What letters seem especially important to him or her? What else do you see besides letters?*

NEXT, invite students to sign their own names, either in manuscript or cursive (many students will already know how to write their names in cursive). Have them try a few different signatures, playing with the "look."

LAST, each student can sign his or her name on one large sheet of butcher paper. You might display students' signatures on a bulletin board.

4 The Longest Word in the World

Students play with the concept of connected letters.

GROUP SIZE: WHOLE GROUP

MATERIALS chalkboard, chalk

FIRST, ask students if they know any long words. Write their responses in manuscript on the board in cursive. (You might also include words such as *antidisestablishmentarianism, Mississippi,* or even nonsense words.)

NEXT, challenge students to guess how many times you will have to pick up your chalk to write each one of those words in cursive. Then write the first word on the board and wait a few minutes before proceeding. Help students understand that you lifted the chalk only nine times when you wrote *antidisestablishmentarianism* because, in cursive, the letters in a word are always connected. You had to lift the chalk one time to write the word and eight more times to dot each of the five *i*'s and cross each of the three *t*'s in the word.

LAST, continue the exercise with the other long words children dictated.

5 Loopy Letters

Students explore similarities between letters, interacting with and observing their forms.

GROUP SIZE: WHOLE GROUP

MATERIALS one copy of page 85 for each student, colored pencils

FIRST, write the following letters in cursive (unconnected) on the board, one set at a time: *b, e, h, k, l,* and, next, *g, j, p, q, y, z*. Last, write *f*.

NEXT, ask students what all the letters have in common. (The first group has loops above the write-on line, the second below, and the *f* above and below.)

LAST, distribute page 85. Invite students to color in the loops. You might have them choose random colors, or help them choose colors that match the letters (lemon yellow for *l*, purple for *p*, green for *g*) or an object the letter represents (orange *b* for basketball, red *h* for hot, and so on). Or, for upward loops, they might choose blue like the sky; for downward loops, brown or green for the earth.

6 Cursive Concentration

Students build visual memory and letter recognition skills, connecting manuscript letters to their cursive forms.

GROUP SIZE: SMALL GROUPS

MATERIALS copies of pages 86–87, construction paper, glue, scissors

FIRST, make a copy of the game for each small group and glue each sheet to a piece of construction paper (so that the cards will not be transparent). When the glue is dry, students can cut along the lines and keep the set of cards together.

NEXT, divide the class into small groups and give one set of playing cards to each group. Invite each group to shuffle the cards and place them all facedown, in even rows, on the floor or table.

LAST, instruct students to take turns turning over two cards at a time, trying to make a cursive-manuscript match (for instance, *a* and a). If the letters do not match, they turn them back over in the same place. If they make a match, they take the two cards and another turn. The player with the most cards at the end wins. Later, you might make a capital version of this game.

ESL/ELD Connection
The playing cards may be used as flashcards by students who are unfamiliar with the English alphabet to help them become more familiar with the letters.

a b c d e f g h i j k l m n o p q r s t u v w x y z

7 Riding the Cursive Wave

Students observe letter shapes and lines, top/bottom orientation, and "negative space."

GROUP SIZE: WHOLE GROUP

MATERIALS two colors of chalk (one blue, if possible), chalkboard

FIRST, write the following letters, words, and sentences in cursive on the board. Ask: *If these sentences were floating or beginning to sink, where would the water go; what would get wet first?*

water

Water i t u w e

wave wet surfing

Water, water, everywhere!

Ride the cursive wave

Cursive Titanic!

Floating Letters Script Ship

NEXT, demonstrate the concept by coloring in the "bottoms" of some letters, words, and sentences.

LAST, invite volunteers to come to the board to color the space below the letters. You might also write some students' names on the board and invite them to color underneath.

ESL/ELD Connection This activity provides a relaxing opportunity to observe letter and word shapes, and expand vocabulary relating to water. Review with students the meanings of any unfamiliar words.

8 Brush Off!

Students make the basic gross-motor strokes that form all cursive letters.

GROUP SIZE: SMALL GROUPS

MATERIALS old newspapers, thick paintbrushes for each student, paint in different colors, paper plates

FIRST, gather each group on the floor or a large surface that can get messy. Provide each student with a small stack of newspaper sheets and distribute different colors of paint on paper plates.

NEXT, write the following strokes on the board very large. Tell students that these five strokes are the basic "building blocks" of cursive, and that as they practice them and learn to put them together, they'll be on their way to writing in cursive!

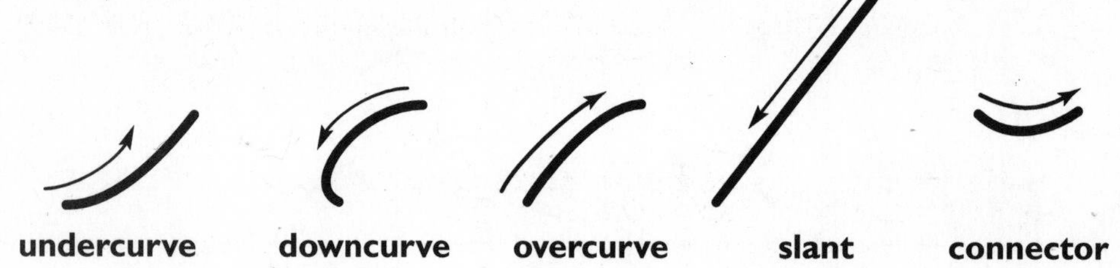

LAST, invite each student to try making the strokes one at a time with his or her paint and paintbrush on the newspaper. They should use a different color for each and move in the direction indicated above. Encourage students to make large strokes and concentrate on the "big feel" of each one, focusing on how their arms and hands move, rather than making it look like any particular letter. Some students may already be able to write their names in cursive; after they try the big strokes, they might experiment with any letters they wish.

9 Read Me

Students learn that they already have the skills to assess cursive writing.

GROUP SIZE: INDIVIDUALS

MATERIALS one copy of page 88 per student, pencils

FIRST, distribute page 88. Ask students to work independently to decide which word or words in each line are the easiest to read.

NEXT, after a few minutes, begin a discussion. Ask: *Which word in the first line was easiest to read? Why?* Introduce students to the terms *slant, shape, size, smoothness,* and *spacing* as they critique each sample (see pages 14–15). For instance, you might say: *The letters are pointing all over the place, so the slant is wrong.*

LAST, encourage students to label each example line with the key descriptors as noted above. Tell them to keep this page in their notebooks for reference.

10. Letter Match

Students begin to recognize and identify cursive letters and connect them to their manuscript forms.

GROUP SIZE: INDIVIDUALS

MATERIALS one copy of pages 89 and 90 per student, a variety of colored pencils or crayons for each student

FIRST, invite students to match up the whole alphabet, cursive to manuscript. Begin with the lowercase letters (p. 89) and then distribute the capital letter sheet (p. 90). Most students will be able to do this easily. As they work, encourage students to notice how the letters are the same and how they are different.

NEXT, when they are finished, have students circle certain cursive letters in different colors. (Some letters will get circled in two colors.) Tell them to:

1. Circle all the cursive letters that appeal to them in red. (For instance, students may think that lowercase *m* looks like fun to write.)
2. Circle all cursive letters that look very similar to their manuscript counterparts in green (*a*, *c*, and *d* are good examples).
3. Circle all cursive letters that look very different from their manuscript counterparts in blue (capitals *Q* and *Z* are good examples).

LAST, have students circle the cursive letters they already know how to write.

11 Height Chart

Students observe that letters are of varying heights and manipulate letters to form words.

GROUP SIZE:
INDIVIDUALS • PARTNERS

MATERIALS copies of pages 91–92, scissors

FIRST, give each student or pair a copy of both pages and let them cut out the letter cards along the dotted lines. They should then mix up all the letter cards.

NEXT, point out that letters are of different heights. Have students sort their letter cards onto appropriate rows on the Height Chart. Guide them to understand that *i* will be the only letter of "medium" height, and that *f* and *j* are exceptional in that they are the only "underwater" letters that rise above the dashed middle line.

LAST, challenge students to use all their "short" letters to form words. List their suggestions on the chalkboard.

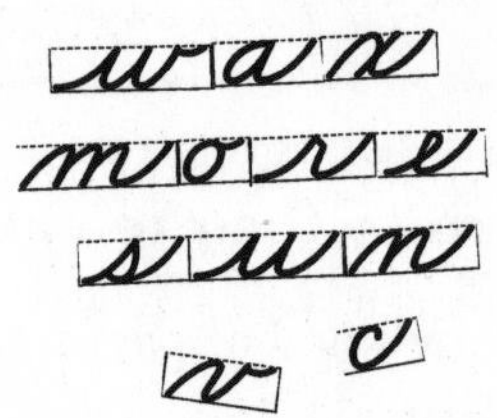

Letter Practice

On the following pages you will find reproducibles for individual writing practice. Letters are divided into groups based on similarity of formation. Go in the order in which they are presented; the practice will build on itself!

Hints for Cursive Instruction

Slant and Grip Begin by helping each student understand proper slant and grip:

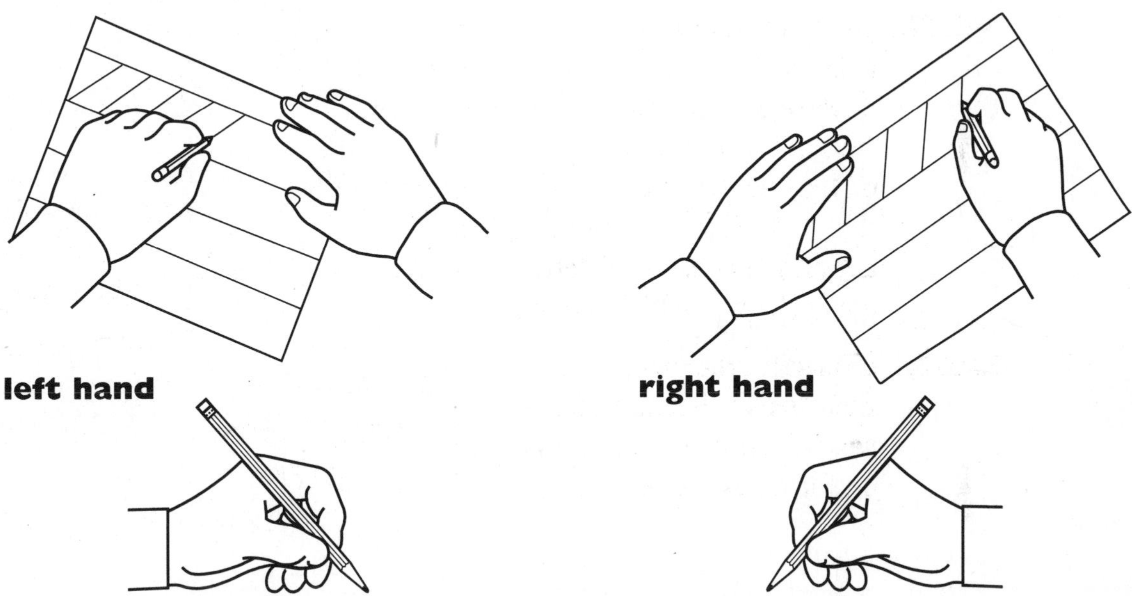

Pencils Medium-soft, standard-sized pencils will probably be the most comfortable for students learning cursive. You might want to give out small "eraser tops" as you begin letter practice. Lots of erasing with a dry or worn-out eraser can be frustrating!

Paper The letter practice pages in this book are reproducible; however, when students begin writing in cursive outside of these pages, a paper with ½-inch lines, red base line, dotted midline, and decender line are recommended. In addition, paper should be positioned at a slant for both manuscript and cursive writing. The slant should nearly parallel the writing arm. For left-handed students, the paper should slant from the right at the top to the left at the bottom.

Can I Sharpen My Pencil?

It is tempting for students to want to keep the sharpest point possible as they create their new letters. But the line for the pencil sharpener—and the disruption it can cause—can be distracting! Five easy management strategies for the "sharpener shuffle" include:

- ✎Make pencil sharpening a morning ritual only: as students get settled, they should sharpen at least three pencils for the day's use.
- ✎Have students bring in small, inexpensive, hand-operated, non-electric sharpeners and do their sharpening at their desks.
- ✎Provide two or more quiet electric sharpeners and put them in different corners of the room to cut down on line time.
- ✎When students do go to the sharpener, have them sharpen several pencils at one time.
- ✎Ask students to sharpen their pencils at home.

I tell the children about the three **P**'s: **pencil** (make sure your grip is correct), **posture** (feet on floor, arms resting on desk, elbows just off desk), and **paper** (make sure it's slanted correctly).

—Jennifer Levin Boss, Elementary School, Hollywood, Florida

General Letter Practice Procedures

These five steps should guide all the letter practice in this section:

1. First, preview the letter you will introduce on the board before passing out the practice sheet. Then give each child a copy of the page with the letters you are introducing. (Give out pages one at a time, staying in order.)
2. Together, examine the letters students will be practicing. Slowly demonstrate each letter on the board as you tell the letter's "story" (found at the beginning of each practice row).
3. Next, have students "air trace" each letter holding their thumb and first two fingers together and forming the new letter in the air, as you tell the "story" again.
4. Then, ask students to pick up their pencils and try one letter on the line provided on their paper. Monitor progress, checking to see that students have understood the basic strokes. If they haven't, take each student's hand in yours and, one by one, guide it through the strokes.
5. Invite students to complete one row of the letter, compare it to the model, and circle their best letter in the row. Once they have mastered the letter, they can move on to practicing letter joinings in the "Connect It!" section of each page.

Cursive Folders Have students designate a folder to hold all their finished practice sheets.

Large Letter Practice Having students use the chalkboard or whiteboard is ideal for beginning letter practice. They can see large letters at eye level and use gross motor movements to form their new letters. Writing on the board can also be less tiresome on the hands and eyes. As you teach each letter, you might invite several students to practice their rows on the board.

Hand-held "linemakers" are available in teacher supply stores to help you make practice lines quickly and evenly. You might also consider putting masking tape on the board to mark "permanent" writing lines.

Cut-Out Letter Cards In the back of the book starting on page 99, students are invited to complete a "perfect" letter card. After each letter page is completed, students should circle a letter as the example of their best work, then complete the letter card, cut it out, and keep it in a neat pile with a rubber band or paper clip. They should cut out the cards as they go along, keeping what will eventually become a stack of fifty-two cards. Many activities in the section that follows will involve these cards.

Reproducible Stationery The stationery on pages 95 and 96 can be used to inspire writing practice while providing built-in letter models.

Name ______________________________

Mountain Climbers

About half of all lowercase cursive letters are Mountain Climbers. You have to climb uphill to begin!

Follow the path with your finger.

Trace and Write

Climb up halfway,
then slide down.
Dot your **i**,
with something round.

Climb uphill,
close to the top.
Slide back down,
but don't you stop.
You're not quite done,
as you can see,
till you put a line,
across your **t**!

Connect It!

The Color Code
Trace all your uphill curves green.

Name ______________________________

a b c d e f g h i j k l m n o p q r s t u v w x y z

u u w w e e

Circle these words in the box.

wet ewe it
tie wit tee
we

e	l	b	i	l
w	w	e	t	f
l	e	w	i	t
i	t	e	e	b

Trace and Write

Climb up **u**,
to the halfway line.
Slide back down,
and up one more time.

u u

Climb up **w**,
just like *u*.
But dip down twice,
Like a *u* times two!

w w

Climb up **e**,
and loop around.
Swoop down and up,
and graze the ground.

e e

Connect It!

eeeeee we

wet tee

wit tie

tut

Holding Hands, Holding Feet! Circle where letters join together. Letters like *w* always hold hands; others, like *e* and *u*, "hold feet"!

Name ______________________________ **Mountain Climbers**

a b c d e f g h i j k l m n o p q r s t u v w x y z

l *l* b *b*

Use the letters you know to finish the puzzle.

i t u w e

Across

1. A spider's house

3. A dollar ____

4. You use your teeth to ____

5. A large animal with horns

6. You take a bath in a ____

Down

2. You use a ____ to hold up your pants.

3. Something that rings

5. The color of the sky

Trace and Write

Climb up long,
and loop down low.
Lovely **l**,
lean and narrow.

l l

Climb up to the top,
loop down and tuck in.
Hold out your hand,
and words can **b**egin!

b b

Connect It!

lll bbb let

be bill

little

blue

Size Check Remember that these letters come all the way to the top line. Are your *b* and *l* the right height? ☐ yes ☐ no

Name ______________________

a b c d e f g h i j k l m n o p q r s t u v w x y z

h *h* k *k*

Unscramble these words and draw a line to match them to their manuscript partners. Write your answers in cursive on the lines. Notice **h** and **k**.

het	the
telb	kite
ettlil	kettle
htete	belt
teltek	teeth
itek	little

Trace and Write

Climb up and climb down,
the whole height you'll fill.
Then add a hump,
because **h** has a hill.

h h *h*

Climb up the **k**,
and drop straight down.
k has a tummy,
and a little ball gown.

k k *k*

Connect It!

hhh *kkk*

hill *hike*

wheel *he*

the

Spaced Out! Look at the spaces between each letter. Are they about the same size? ☐ yes ☐ no

Name ______________________

a b c d e f g h i j k l m n o p q r s t u v w x y z

r r s s

i t w u e
l b h k

Use the letters you already know to form the words.

sit sit wire r

hills s kites s

stir s r three r

Trace and Write

Climb up **r**,
stop halfway.
Run to the right,
then race away!

r r

Climb up **s**,
stop halfway.
Tuck in and under,
and sail away!

s s

Connect It!

rrr sss

is rise

sir

see

Check Your Slant Look at your words. Which way do your letters slant? Any slant is okay, but the letters should all slant in one direction!

- ☐ forward
- ☐ backward
- ☐ straight up
- ☐ all mixed up

Name ______________________________

a b c d e f g h i j k l m n o p q r s t u v w x y z

f f p p j j

Which of these letters can you find in the scribble? Trace over them with a highlighter.

i t w u e l b
h k r s f p j

Trace and Write

Climb up **f**,
the longest of all.
The higher the climb,
the deeper the fall.

Climb up **p**,
peak up and down.
Make a loop,
pop off the ground.

Climb up **j**,
then journey down.
Jump on out,
the dot's my crown.

Connect It!

fff ppp
jjj feet
jeep up
few

Shape Up! Check your shape. Do your letters close up where they should? Are they too thin or wide?

Name ______________________

a b c d e f g h i j k l m n o p q r s t u v w x y z

a a d d g g

Downhill Daredevils

There are six lowercase letters that start with a round downhill stroke. Downhill Daredevils head down steep curves backward!

Follow their path with your finger.

a d g

Trace and Write

Attention all autos!
Loop back all the way.
Now you're ready,
to close up **a**.

a a a

Dash down **d**,
Then up a bit.
Drop down to the ground,
and make a dip!

d d d

Slide down and close up,
then down you go.
Gain some speed,
and watch **g** grow!

g g g

Connect It!

aaa ddd

ggg as

dare slide

glad

The Color Code Trace all our downhill curves in brown crayon. Pretend you're on a dirtbike!

Name

a b c d e f g h i j k l m n o p q r s t u v w x y z

q *q* o *o* c *c*

Hand Holders

You know **b** and **w**, now meet **o**. These letters need to hold hands with the next letter! (The last hand-holder, **v**, is coming right up!)

Circle wherever hands hold.

wobble

Trace and Write

Slide down **q**,
close it tight.
Dive down quite deep,
then tuck him in right!

q q q

Slide down little **o**,
sitting neatly on land.
o needs someone,
to hold her hand.

o o o

Cars cruise backward,
down curvy **c**.
They climb back up,
then **c** is free.

c c c

Connect It!

qu *ooo*

ccc *race*

quick *or*

go

Smooth Move Look at your "lines." Are they too heavy, too light, or all mixed up? Make sure they're even.

☐ too heavy ☐ too light ☐ all mixed up ☐ just right!

Name

a b c d e f g h i j k l m n o p q r s t u v w x y z

n *n* m *m* v *v*

Lumpy Letters

Your last six lowercase cursive letters are lumpy! They go uphill and curve over. Look at these lumps:

n m v x y z

These are easy to confuse! Here's a way to remember them. You draw a nest in n, turn m into mountains, and make v into a valley.

n m v

Trace and Write

Lump up and over,
down again.
Repeat that and,
you've got an **n**.

n 1 2 *n*

Lump up and over,
m is me.
n has 2 lumps,
I have 3.

m 1 2 3 *m*

A bumpy start,
that's little **v**.
Make a valley and,
hold hands with me.

v 1 2 *v*

Connect It!

nnn *vvv*

mmm *no*

very *in*

van

The Color Code
Trace all your lumps in red!

Name

a b c d e f g h i j k l m n o p q r s t u v w x y z

x *x* y *y* z *z*

Did you know . . .

x

...the expression "**x** marks the spot" comes from an old practice of burying treasure and marking the ground so that someone else can find it?

y

...is a vowel *and* a consonant?

z

...in England, **z** is called "zed"?

Trace and Write

Lump up and over,
up again.
Cross your **x**,
and that's the end.

x x x

y is a *u*,
with a tail of a *g*.
Pour in the top,
yummy cocoa for me!

y y y

z looks like,
a funny *3*,
zipping and zooming,
and very zany!

z z z

Connect It!

xxx *xyz*

zzz *x-ray*

lumpy *ox*

zoo

Tic-Tac-Toe Now that you know **x**, play cursive tic-tac-toe with a friend. You might also use u/w, l/b, g/q, i/t, e/l, h/k, b/d, n/m, w/v, y/j.

a b c d e f g h i j k l m n o p q r s t u v w x y z

A 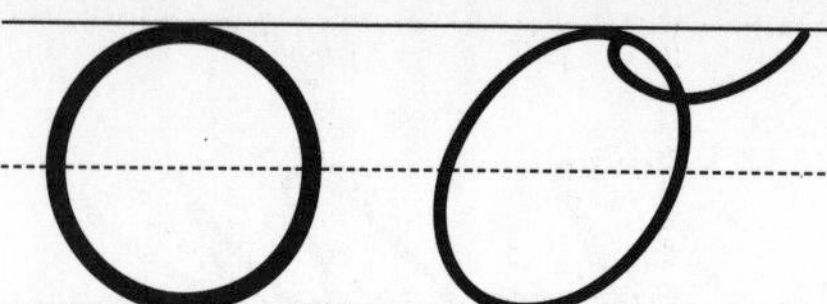 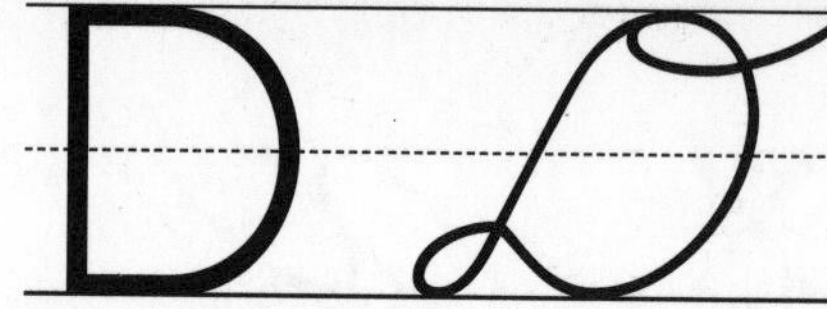

> **Backward Balloons**
> Six cursive capitals look like big, round balloons. The first stroke moves backward.

Color in the balloons.

Trace and Write

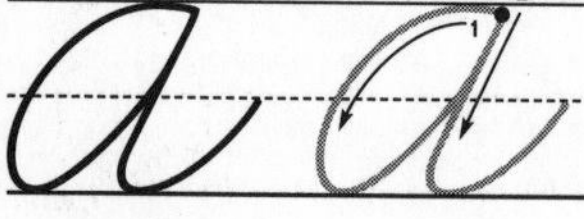 

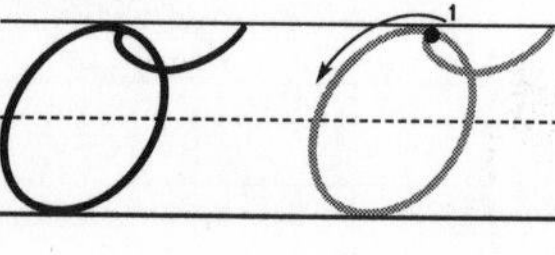 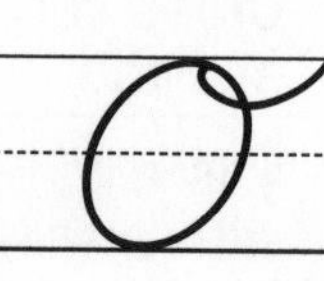

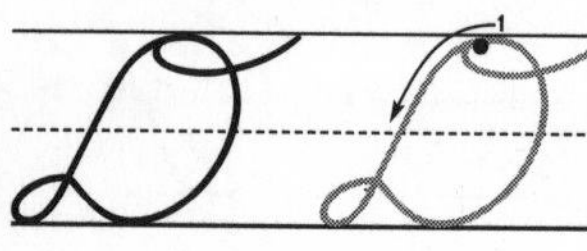 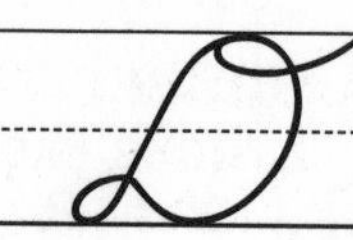

Connect It!
Copy words from this book title.

Otters

Dive

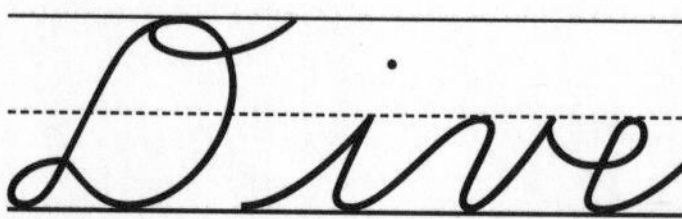

Name ____________________

a b c d e f g h i j k l m n o p q r s t u v w x y z

C C E E Q Q

E looks like a backward 3!

Trace and Write

C C C

E E E

Q Q Q

Connect It!

Copy words from this envelope.

Carl Quinn
205 Elm Street
Easton, Colorado

Carl

Quinn

Elm

Easton

Colorado

Name ____________________

a b c d e f g h i j k l m n o p q r s t u v w x y z

Trace the letters with your finger.

Lefties

With **I** and **J**, the first stroke moves backward to the left.

Trace and Write

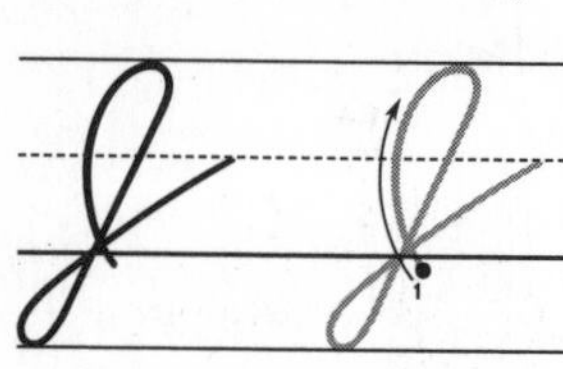

Connect It!

Copy words from this calendar.

Icicles

January

Iowa

Name ______________________________

a b c d e f g h i j k l m n o p q r s t u v w x y z

N *N* M *M* W *W*

Curly Qs

There are 10 cursive capitals that start with a fancy little loop. Look at the loops.

N M W

Trace and Write

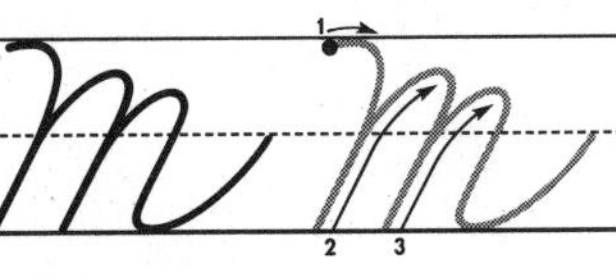

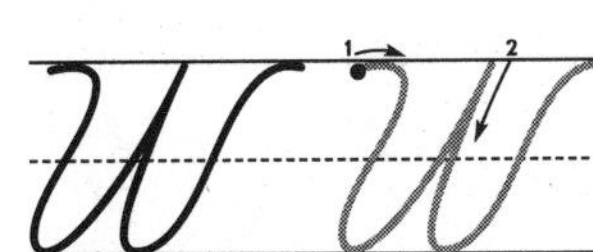

W

Connect It!

Copy state names from this map.

Nevada

Maine

Wyoming

Extra Practice On another sheet of paper, write any five states:

Nebraska, New York, Montana, North Carolina, Massachusetts, Washington, North Dakota, Maryland, West Virginia, New Hampshire, Michigan, Wisconsin, New Jersey, Missouri, Wyoming, New Mexico, Minnesota

Name ______________________ Curly Qs

a b c d e f g h i j k l m n o p q r s t u v w x y z

H H K K X X

Trace and Write

H H H

K K K

X X X

Happy Valentine's Day

Hugs and Kisses xo xo Kim

Connect It!

Copy words from this valentine.

Happy

Hugs

Kisses

XOXO

Kim

Name ________________________________

a b c d e f g h i j k l m n o p q r s t u v w x y z

U U Y Y V V

Trace and Write

U U U

Y Y Y

V V V

A Very Young Unicorn
by Vera Yule

Connect It!
Copy words from this book title.

Very

Young

Unicorn

Vera

Yule

a b c d e f g h i j k l m n o p q r s t u v w x y z

Z z

Trace and Write

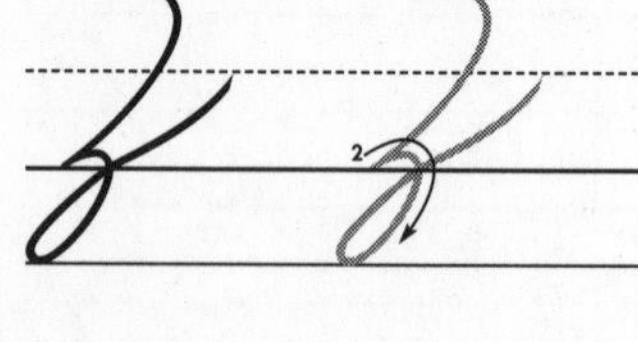

Connect It!

Copy words from this picture book.

Zany

Zebras

Zip

Zippers

Zanzibar

Name Poems!
Write vertical poems using capital letters.

A — Amazing,
N — Never eats peas,
N — Nice,
A — Always Friendly

Name ______________________________________

a b c d e f g h i j k l m n o p q r s t u v w x y z

P P R R B B

Kickstarts

There are three cursive capitals that start with a little kick!

Trace and Write

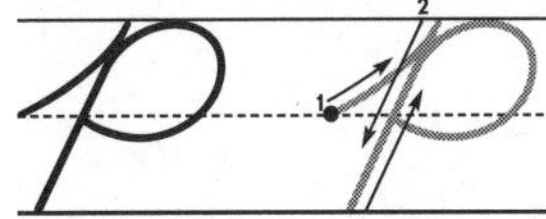

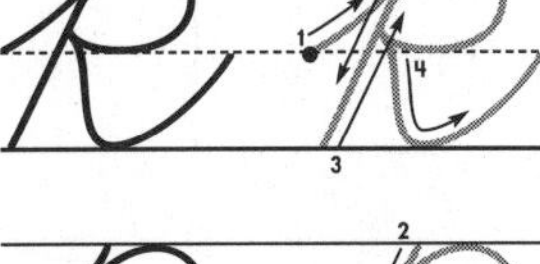

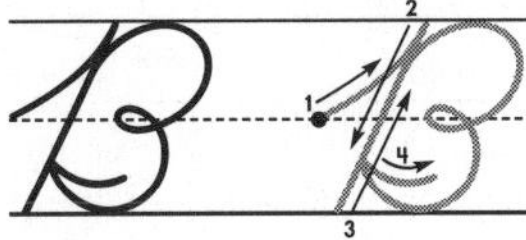

Connect It!

Copy words from this book.

Peanut

Butter

Recipes

Parties

a b c d e f g h i j k l m n o p q r s t u v w x y z

T T F F

Tabletops

T and **F** look like fancy tables!

Draw some food on the T and F tables.

Tabletop Feast

Trace and Write

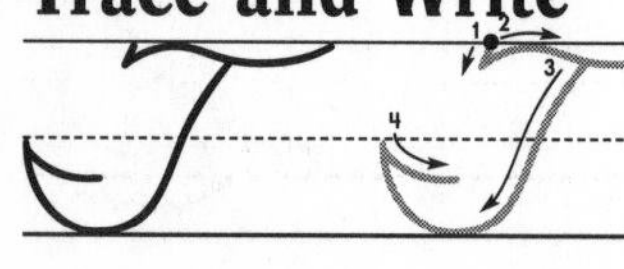

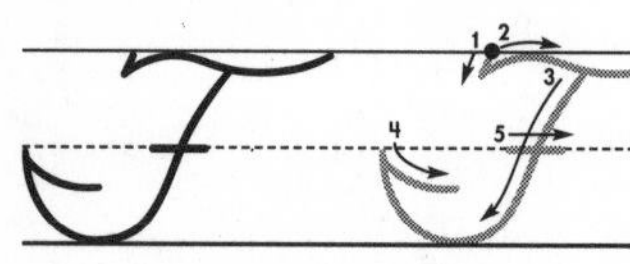

April

Sunday	Monday	Tuesday	Wednesday	Thursday	Friday	Saturday
			1	2	3	4
5	6	7	8	9	10	11

Connect It!
Copy words from this calendar.

Tuesday

Thursday

Friday

Name ______________________________

a b c d e f g h i j k l m n o p q r s t u v w x y z

G G S S L L

Capital Mountains

These are like the Mountain Climbers you started with, but bigger!

Trace and Write

G G G

S S S

L L L

Food List
Grapes
Lemons
Soup

Connect It!

Copy the grocery shopping list.

Grapes

Lemons

Soup

Now you know every cursive capital and lowercase letter! Write a letter to a friend or relative and address the envelope using what you know!

Lee Miller
123 New Street
Anytown, USA

Aa Bb Cc Dd Ee Ff Gg Hh Ii Jj Kk Ll Mm

Nn Oo Pp Qq Rr Ss Tt Uu Vv Ww Xx Yy Zz

Activities for All Learning Modalities

As a teacher, you know that there is a range of learning modalities or styles in your classroom: that visual learners learn best by seeing, physical or kinesthetic learners by doing, tactile learners by touching, and auditory learners by hearing. You probably also suspect that these styles will continue to "show through" as students learn to write in cursive.

You have probably noticed that students do not fit into neat little boxes; there is often overlap between learning styles. While these activities are grouped into learning styles—visual, tactile, physical/kinesthetic, and auditory—remember they are usually appropriate for the whole group. You'll want to give every child a chance to engage in all kinds of activities; combining modalities often leads to faster learning!

Each activity suggests an appropriate group size. When students are working in small groups, you might find it helpful to assign specific roles (materials gatherer, time monitor, and so on). Messy activities are indicated by this icon. Have lots of paper towels or smocks on hand for those!

Where appropriate, tips are provided throughout for additional ways to support those children who are learning English as a second language or who are limited English proficient.

Visual Learners

Visual learners enjoy closely examining, copying, tracing, and highlighting cursive letters. When provided with a clear written model, they are often able to "imprint" that letter into their memory. These students might take naturally to "traditional" handwriting instruction and its independent copying of rows of letters. With their good visual memory and mental imaging strategies, they often ease into this new writing system without much explicit instruction. It is important to remember, however, that visual learners, if left to practice letter forms independently, may be practicing incorrect formations over and over, sealing them in their visual memory! They will benefit from direct instruction and detailed, guided self-assessment, since they may still need to fine-tune their letter forms. The following activities are particularly helpful for visual learners.

12 Script Strips

Students create personalized name tags for their desks.

GROUP SIZE: INDIVIDUALS

MATERIALS oak tag strips; rulers; pencils; markers; crayons; assorted art supplies such as glitter, gold and silver markers

FIRST, write each student's name in cursive (using pencil) on an oak tag strip. (Draw a bottom, top, and middle line in pencil with a ruler.)

NEXT, give students their strips. Have them trace over their names using art supplies.

LAST, have students decorate their strips and tape them to their desks.

13 Red Light, Green Light

Students observe the beginnings and endings of individual letters and look at confusing joinings.

GROUP SIZE: INDIVIDUALS

MATERIALS red and green pencils, markers, or chalk; or small red and green stickers cut into tiny pieces; letter practice sheets (any from pages 28–47)

FIRST, as students practice their new letters on the letter practice sheets, point out beginnings and endings of each letter. Explain to students that some joinings of letters can be confusing to write. Write *bit*, *on*, *vow*, *we*, *yoyo*, and *vine* on the board and ask volunteers to draw dots on the beginning points of each word in green chalk and the ending points of each letter in red chalk.

solid dot = red chalk
open circle = green chalk

bit on vow

NEXT, distribute the pencils, markers, or stickers and ask students to put a green mark at the beginning of each letter on their practice sheet and a red one at the end. As they practice connecting the letters at the bottom of the sheet, have students mark letter "joinings" in red.

solid dot = red chalk
open circle = green chalk

bit on vow

LAST, have students add their sheets to their cursive folders for reference.

14 Wild Writing

Students focus on the shapes and lines of letters with bright, engaging colors.

GROUP SIZE:
INDIVIDUALS • PARTNERS

MATERIALS fluorescent markers; gold, silver, and copper-colored thick and thin markers (available in craft and stationery stores); white, unlined paper

FIRST, make sure students have clear models of each letter.

NEXT, invite students to use the markers to write letters on white paper. They may do this in many ways, but model the technique of writing in a florescent color and tracing the outside of the letters with the metallic hue (or vice versa). Remind students that they may find it helpful to make their model in pencil first.

LAST, when they have practiced several individual letters, have students write their name, if possible, or words from their letter practice pages. If they can write all their letters, students might enjoy making signs for their room or desk.

15 Write On!

Students practice letters on a variety of surfaces.

GROUP SIZE:
INDIVIDUALS • PARTNERS

Any of the following can be used for independent or partnered writing practice. Make sure students have a clear model of cursive letters and invite them to practice on:

Write-On/Wipe-Off Boards These small white boards may be one of the most useful and convenient tools for cursive practice. You might even use permanent marker or tape to mark guiding lines onto the board. Provide students with a range of colored write-on/wipe-off markers to use on their boards.

Magna Doodle™ This board is available in most toy stores. It looks a bit like a flat TV screen and uses a round, flat magnet as a writing instrument. Invite students to write large letters, then "erase" their attempts.

Magic Slate™ This inexpensive "slate," available in most toy stores, involves a transparent sheet and pencil-like writing instrument. After students write on the slate, they lift the transparent sheet to erase their work.

16 Hangman

Students anticipate how cursive letters are connected and use their knowledge to predict whole words and word configurations.

GROUP SIZE: WHOLE GROUP

MATERIALS chalkboard, chalk

FIRST, explain to students that they will be playing a different version of hangman. Think of a word or sentence for the game. You might choose a word from your weekly spelling or vocabulary list. Even if students have not learned all the letters in the word or sentence, they will begin to anticipate new letter shapes.

NEXT, have students guess letters and play hangman by the traditional rules, but fill in the blanks with cursive letters that clearly show the connections to the next letter. Students may be able to guess letters based on their beginning strokes.

c _ r _ _ v e

LAST, continue the game with as many words as time permits.

17 Spelling Bee Scrambles

Students manipulate cut-out letter cards and focus on letter joinings.

GROUP SIZE: WHOLE GROUP

MATERIALS cut-out letter cards (pages 100–111), pencil and paper

FIRST, have students place their letter cards faceup on their desks.

NEXT, say a word from the weekly spelling or vocabulary list and ask students to pick out the letters to spell out the word on their desks.

LAST, ask a volunteer to arrange his or her cards on the ledge of the board so the class can check their spelling. All students should then write the word in cursive on a piece of paper. As a twist, you might have students work in pairs to make "scrambles" for each other: one student can mix up and lay out the letters that form a word and the other can unscramble them.

18 A Rainbow of Difference

Students observe confusing similarities between letters and highlight their differences.

GROUP SIZE: INDIVIDUALS

MATERIALS highlighters or colored pencils, lined paper

FIRST, ask students to write in cursive the following letter pairs side by side: l/b, h/k, n/m, u/w, u/v, and any other pair they think looks similar.

NEXT, ask students to choose two colors and trace over the strokes of the letters that are similar in one color, and the strokes that are different in another.

l b

— **different**
— **same**

LAST, ask volunteers to share any additional letter pairs they wrote and discuss their similarities and differences with the class.

19 Change Over!

Students trace over manuscript words in cursive, observing letter similarities and differences and focusing on whole words.

GROUP SIZE: INDIVIDUALS • PARTNERS

MATERIALS oak tag strips, marker, pencils

FIRST, write your weekly vocabulary words or spelling list in manuscript on each piece of oak tag with marker.

NEXT, give each student or pair one strip. Have them trace over the manuscript letters with cursive ones. They might finger-trace first.

LAST, keep all strips in a "vocabulary" or "spelling" box. Students might alphabetize the strips.

cursive

20 Alphabet Books

Students practice each letter by writing an alphabet book (a genre that usually uses only manuscript letters) and associate pictures with letters.

GROUP SIZE: INDIVIDUALS • PARTNERS

MATERIALS unlined, 8½-inch by 11-inch white paper (eight sheets per book); crayons, markers, or colored pencils; stapler; art supplies such as glue and glitter; scissors; magazines to cut up

FIRST, discuss alphabet books and display some examples. Many students will remember books they read in kindergarten or first grade, such as *Alligators All Around* by Maurice Sendak or *Eating the Alphabet* by Lois Ehlert.

NEXT, invite students to rewrite their favorite alphabet book (you might take a class trip to the library to select them) or write their own, this time using cursive. If they choose to rewrite an existing book, an especially fun one is *Chicka Chicka Boom Boom* by John Archambault, in which all 26 letters become tangled together in a tree. If they choose to create their own, encourage students to think of a theme. (Friends, nature, animals, our community, desserts, and "this year in our class" all work well.) Have them make a list of what will be on each page, letter by letter. They may choose one word per page ("a: apple") or an entire sentence ("a: Artichokes are grown in California."). When students get stuck on *x,* provide them with examples, such as "*x* marks the spot where ____," xylophone, XL (extra large), x-ray, xi (a Greek letter), xerox, or words that begin with *ex* such as *extra, exactly, exceptional, excellent, exam, exciting, expand, expect,* and *express*.

ESL/ELD Connection

Students who lack basic classroom vocabulary can benefit from making "school ABC books" including vocabulary they will need or use immediately. A suggested list:

a alphabet; **b** bus, boy; **c** cafeteria, crayon; **d** desk, door; **e** eraser, everyone; **f** friend; **g** girl, going home; **h** help, hopscotch; **i** I have a question; **j** jump rope; **k** kid; **l** lunch; **m** Mr./Ms. (teacher's name); **n** nurse; **o** one, two, three...; **p** paper, pencil, please; **q** quiet; **r** recess, red; **s** school, students; **t** teacher, thank you; **u** understand; **v** very good; **w** What page are we on? Where is it?; **x** X marks the spot; **y** yesterday; **z** zip code.

THEN, show students how to make a book: take eight sheets of paper and put them in a neat pile. Fold the pile in half and staple the folded edge. They will have a book with enough pages for the whole alphabet, plus a front and back cover, "the end" page, and dedication page.

LAST, let students work on their books, writing the capital and lowercase form of each letter on a page. Students might enjoy presenting their finished products to younger siblings or students in other classes or grades who have not yet started learning cursive!

21 Speed Bingo

Students develop quick letter-recognition skills.

GROUP SIZE: INDIVIDUALS • PARTNERS

MATERIALS cut-out letter cards (pages 100–111), bingo chips, small sticky notes or pennies

FIRST, have students place five rows of five letters on their desks in any arrangement, leaving a "free" space in the middle (they can simply turn one card over).

NEXT, play bingo. Write manuscript letters randomly and quickly on the board. Students must put a markers on the corresponding cursive letters until someone calls "bingo."

LAST, have students rearrange their cards and play again!

22 Book Covers

Students practice using capital letters for a common purpose.

GROUP SIZE: INDIVIDUALS • PARTNERS

MATERIALS scrap paper, pencils, large paper bags or butcher paper, masking tape, magic markers, crayons, pencils

FIRST, help students find books that need covers. Remind students that most of the words in book titles and authors'/illustrators' names are capitalized. Have students examine the book they will be covering to see where the title is written, and write down the title and author of their book on a scrap piece of paper.

NEXT, help students cover their books with paper and make lines in pencil to guide their writing.

LAST, have students create their book covers. They can illustrate them and write summaries of the books on the back covers if they like.

23 Cursive Calendar

Students create calendars for home use.

GROUP SIZE: INDIVIDUALS

MATERIALS twelve copies of page 93 for each student, art supplies (old magazines, decorative materials, photographs from home—remind students to get permission for these, and so on), posterboard or construction paper, stapler or glue

FIRST, distribute twelve copies of the calendar sheet on page 93 to each student. (Alternatively, you might do just one month, or the remaining months of the school year.)

NEXT, have students label the month and days of the week properly in cursive. Provide them with a model to fill in the numbered days for each month.

LAST, have students decorate their calendars however they like, perhaps with drawings or photographs. They might add birthdays, vacations, class events or assignments, and holidays. Staple or glue each stack aligned with the top on a large piece of oak tag or construction paper.

Math Link As students mark their calendar with the days of the month, focus on counting by sevens.

ESL/ELD Connection
Students can learn months and days of the week in English, or create a calendar in their first language to share with the class.

Tactile Learners

Tactile learners learn best by incorporating their sense of touch into their cursive experience. Touching, tracing and retracing, feeling, and physically interacting with the letters will all help tactile learners. These students will often "key in" to a letter by exploring it through texture and shape. The following activities are intended to support tactile learners.

24 Glitter Templates

Students create and feel "raised" letters.

GROUP SIZE:
INDIVIDUALS • SMALL GROUPS

MATERIALS marker, large index cards, glue, Q-tips, glitter in different colors (you might also use sand), yarn in two different colors, drinking straws cut into small pieces, scissors

FIRST, using a marker, write one letter on each card (draw lines on the card as shown below) and distribute the cards evenly to students. Provide each group with a glue supply (one large plate of glue with several Q-tips, or a small container of glue for each child working at the table), yarn, scissors, pieces of straw, and several colors of glitter.

NEXT, invite students to create letter cards. They can trace over each letter in glue and then sprinkle on glitter or sand. When the letter itself is dry, they should then glue yarn on the top and bottom lines (using different colors for each) and the straws on the dotted line in the middle.

LAST, when glue has dried, have students close their eyes and try to "read" each other's letters with their fingers. You might want to discuss the Braille alphabet with the group.

It will be helpful to use these cards as new letters are introduced. Have students "feel" the letter with their eyes open, then closed, then open again. They will then be ready to write the letter.

This exercise may be repeated with the uppercase alphabet.

25 Line in the Sand

Students practice writing in a fun medium.

GROUP SIZE: INDIVIDUALS • PARTNERS

MATERIALS plastic containers with lots of surface area or shoe boxes, sand, water, sticks, shells, coins, cut-up strips of old beach towels

FIRST, create miniature sandboxes for the classroom by filling several large, flat, shallow plastic containers with sand. (Shoe boxes will work well but won't last as long.)

NEXT, add a little water to each box, enough to make the sand resemble the texture found at the beach, where you can write with a stick. Invite students to choose their "pencil": their fingers, sticks, or actual pencils.

LAST, have students practice writing letters and short words in their sandboxes. Add shells or coins ("treasure") to each box for dotting *i*'s and cut-up strips of an old beach towel for crossing *t*'s!

26 Cursive Buffet

Students practice letters with tasty writing tools.

In these activities, students not only see, feel, and manipulate letters, they also taste them! The following activities are appropriate to use after new letters are introduced, or for additional practice anytime.

Depending on students' mastery of the letters, a clear model or template will be helpful in each activity. (You might write in permanent marker on waxed paper or aluminum foil.)

Licorice Have students practice writing letters or words using red and black shoestring licorice. Provide them with long pieces of licorice and clean sheets of paper or paper onto which a letter has been traced. They might glue the licorice onto the paper, or eat the letters when they are finished.

Melted Chocolate Melt a large bag of semisweet chocolate chips in a saucepan or microwave oven. When chips are melted and cool enough to handle, divide the mixture into paper cups or small dishes and provide small groups of students with sheets of waxed paper. Invite students to take a big "blob" of melted chocolate onto their index finger and paint letters or short words onto the waxed paper. (They may have to add more chocolate and retrace the letters and their connections in order to make them thick enough so that, after chilling, they can break off in one piece.) They might even decorate their letters with colored sprinkles! Place the sheets of waxed paper in the refrigerator or freezer for at least ten minutes. When students have claimed their sheets, have them gently peel off the waxed paper from the chocolate letters. Have a cursive chocolate party!

Cake Decorating Students can practice their writing with cake-decorating tubes full of frosting and screw-on plastic tops (available at supermarkets). Discuss why the writing on cakes is often done in cursive, what special challenges cake decorators might face in their task, and what is usually seen on cakes, such as *Happy Birthday, Congratulations,* and so on. Have students practice their technique in small groups using waxed paper or aluminum foil. Are there any special occasions in the classroom for which they might decorate a cake? Later, you might make or purchase several frosted cakes for them to decorate as their finished product. You might also consider inviting a local baker or pastry chef (perhaps a parent has these skills) in for a demonstration.

Squeeze Cheese Divide the class into small groups and provide each group with large sheets of waxed paper or aluminum foil and a can of squeeze cheese (available in supermarkets). Challenge them to write certain words or letters on waxed paper using the cheese. (Expect some giggles as they get the hang of handling the can!) This is one medium that allows students to easily write longer words or even sentences. They might enjoy dipping crackers into their finished work before eating it.

Sweet Script Use plastic honey containers with tops that allow you to squirt the honey out. Invite students to squirt out certain letters or words onto aluminum foil. They may enjoy dipping apple slices into their words before eating them.

Cursive Cookies

1½ sticks softened butter
¾ cup sugar
1 egg
½ tsp. vanilla
2 cups flour
¼ tsp. baking powder
¼ tsp. salt
food coloring (optional)
a little milk to brush on top

Decorations:
sprinkles, colored sugar, silver balls, and so on

Cream together butter and sugar. Add egg and vanilla, mixing well. Gradually add the flour, baking powder, and salt; mix well. Divide dough into four parts (add a drop of food-coloring to each if you want), wrap closely in plastic wrap, and chill 30 minutes until it is the consistency of modeling clay. Have four groups of students roll out long ropes of dough on waxed paper. Students can form cursive letters or words, decorating their letters however they want. They might also write their names or see how many connected letters can stay together through the baking process. Bake at 375°F on an ungreased sheet for about 10 minutes.

ESL/ELD Connection Encourage children to participate in any of the Cursive Buffet activities by spelling out some of their native language food words and their English translations and sharing them with the class.

Alphabet Soup Share a bag or box of alphabet soup letters (available in the pasta section of most large supermarkets) with the group. Ask children to grab a handful of letters, pick out the ones they've learned to write in cursive, and practice writing those letters, one row of each. Then challenge them to make words out of their letters and see if they can write out their creations in cursive.

Spaghetti Script Provide each student or small group with a handful of raw spaghetti (any thickness or type will work: spaghetti, vermicelli, angel hair, spaghettini, fettucini, and so on, though the thinner the better) and waxed paper or aluminum foil. Challenge them to write letters or their name without breaking up the raw spaghetti. Next, boil the spaghetti until it is somewhat overcooked. Give each child or group a small "nest" of spaghetti, this time challenging them to write the same letters they tried with the raw spaghetti. (Some letters will be very easy to write with one string of spaghetti, such as *e, l,* and *f,* others will require using two pieces, such as *j, p,* and *w*. Remind students they will have to break up their pieces of pasta as needed.) When they are finished, ask students to describe and compare each writing experience. Which was easier? Faster? More fun? Which looked more appealing to them?

27 Shaving Cream Script

Students practice letters with all their fingers in a three-dimensional medium.

GROUP SIZE: INDIVIDUALS • PARTNERS

MATERIALS waxed paper or aluminum foil, tape, shaving cream (one can) (You might also try this activity with fingerpaint.)

FIRST, give each child a sheet of waxed paper large enough to cover the length of his or her desk and four pieces of tape to secure the corners. When sheets are taped down, squirt onto the center of each student's sheet a mound of shaving cream a little smaller than a tennis ball.

NEXT, invite students to use their hands to spread the cream into a thin layer all over their waxed paper.

LAST, have them practice writing letters or words onto their surface, using different fingers, and "clearing" their slate after each writing attempt!

28 Back and Palm Writing

Students physically "receive" a letter and use gross-motor movements to form a letter without visual input.

GROUP SIZE: PARTNERS • THREES

MATERIALS cut-out letter cards (pages 100–111) for reference

FIRST, help students divide into partners or threes and sit together. Each group should have the stack of cut-out letter cards. One child will be the writer and the other the reader. (If students are in groups of three, the third observes.)

NEXT, ask the writer to draw one letter in cursive on the reader's back or palm. When the reader guesses correctly (writers or observers may give hints), students switch roles.

LAST, once students have mastered this new medium, invite them to begin forming words.

29 Sponge Writing

Students use water and a sponge to form letters on the board.

GROUP SIZE:
INDIVIDUALS • PARTNERS

MATERIALS sponges of various sizes, chalkboard, chalk (You might also try this with wet paintbrushes.)

FIRST, write several models of letters in chalk along the top of the board. Set a small bowl of water near the chalkboard so that each child can wet his or her sponge.

NEXT, invite students to practice new letters on the board underneath the models with their wet sponges as their writing tool. The water mark will stay for a short time and then disappear. When practicing one particular letter, challenge students to write their "best letter" in the row before the rest disappear.

LAST, invite students to practice writing whole words.

30 Clay Tablets

Students practice letter formation in a fun, three-dimensional medium.

GROUP SIZE:
INDIVIDUALS • PARTNERS • SMALL GROUPS

MATERIALS bulk amount of clay; wax paper (one sheet for each tablet); different writing utensils, such as pencils, pen caps, unbent paper clips

FIRST, distribute a chunk of clay to each student, pair, or small group. Point out to students that clay has been used as a writing surface throughout history. Invite them to flatten the clay onto their waxed paper so that a "tablet" is made.

NEXT, ask students to choose a tool with which to begin writing on their tablet. They may form letters or words and then periodically wipe the slate clean.

THEN, invite students to experiment with all the available writing tools. Are some easier to write with? How do their results vary depending on the type of tool used?

LAST, once they have done their best writing, students may let their clay tablet dry for a permanent writing record.

31 Cursive Bag

Students practice writing in a fun-to-erase medium.

GROUP SIZE:
INDIVIDUALS • PARTNERS

MATERIALS one self-seal plastic bag for each student or pair, a large bottle or tube of clear hair gel, food coloring

FIRST, provide each child or pair with a bag. Have students open their bags as you (or a student volunteer) squirt a bit of clear hair gel the size of a large marble into each bag.

NEXT, add several drops of food coloring to each bag. Students can mix up the gel and food coloring by massaging the bag to make a colored "slate." They should then seal their bags, making sure there is no air trapped inside.

LAST, students can finger-trace letters and words (using their fingertips) onto this fun writing surface. Experiment with different amounts of gel. Depending on how much is inside and how evenly it is distributed, letters may disappear soon after they are made or stay until they are "erased."

32 Cursive Confetti Celebration

Students celebrate cursive in a colorful medium of unusual texture and write for a purpose.

GROUP SIZE:
SMALL GROUPS • WHOLE GROUP

MATERIALS confetti (available at party-supply stores, or homemade with a paper cutter), butcher or banner paper, glue

FIRST, discuss celebrations with the group: *Are any birthdays or holidays coming up? Are congratulations in order for anyone in the school community?* As a group, decide what sign you will make.

NEXT, draw lines onto the paper so that students can write their message in pencil, and help them assess their writing. When writing is legible, have students trace over the pencil in glue.

THEN, have students sprinkle confetti over the letters and shake the paper around a bit so all the glue is covered. Let the banner dry.

LAST, let students admire and touch their work. Display the banner.

33 Cursive Clay

Students practice writing and make signs in a three-dimensional, erasable, and easily manipulated medium.

GROUP SIZE: INDIVIDUALS

MATERIALS polymer clay such as (Fimo or Sculpey™) in a variety of colors (available in most craft or toy stores), conventional oven

FIRST, provide children with a choice of clay. Have them decide what color their background will be, and what they will write on their sign.

NEXT, have students make a flat, simple background. They may then roll the clay into thin ropes and use it to form words in cursive, pressing each word into the background so that it will stick.

LAST, put their work on a cookie sheet and bake (follow instructions on clay packages) to make their cursive signs permanent!

Physical/Kinesthetic Learners

For some learners, experience through gross-motor (large muscle) movement is key to success and memorization, especially when they first experience a new letter. These are kinesthetic (or physical) learners, who will learn new material best by involving their entire bodies. Air-tracing or manipulating large letters, staying physically active as they create letters, and "stretching" their fingers before and after writing will help these learners.

34 Skywriting

Students use their whole arm to form letters.

GROUP SIZE: PARTNERS

MATERIALS cut-out letter cards (pages 100–111) for reference

FIRST, ask partners to sit side by side, facing in the same direction. Have them choose who will "write" first and who will "read." Have them choose five cards from their pile.

NEXT, invite the writer to choose one of the five letters to air-trace. They should hold their fingers as if they were gripping a pencil but use their whole arm and lots of air space to form the letter in the air.

LAST, the reader should guess the letter. After several letters, have students switch roles. They might then try this activity with short words.

35 Sidewalk Chalk

Students use gross-motor movements to form letters outdoors.

GROUP SIZE: SMALL GROUPS

MATERIALS thick pieces of colored sidewalk chalk, cut-out letter cards (pages 100–111) for reference, an outdoor surface

FIRST, divide the class into several small groups and go outside to a sidewalk, playground surface, or any other acceptable outdoor surface (a brick wall that faces the playground, for instance). Have each group choose their own area on which to work. Each group should have one stack of letter cards.

NEXT, let them form letters. Encourage them to create large letters, small ones, wide and narrow ones, short and tall ones. You might also encourage them to decorate their letters as they want, or put them together to form words and sentences, and so on.

LAST, let students walk around to admire the work of the other groups!

ESL/ELD Connection Outdoor activities give students the chance to notice environmental print (street signs, the school sign, and so on). They might try to write what they see in cursive.

36 Body Writing

Students experience letter shapes using their whole body.

GROUP SIZE: SMALL GROUPS

MATERIALS one set of cut-out letter cards (pages 100–111) for reference, a large space in which to move

FIRST, give each group a cut-out letter card.

NEXT, challenge one group at a time, with the rest of the class observing, to find a way to create certain cursive letters with their bodies, either lying flat on the floor or standing up. You might time the groups to see which is able to form letters the fastest.

LAST, to introduce a fun twist, have several groups work together to spell out an entire word with their bodies!

37 Jump It!

Students use gross-motor movements to form letters as part of an energetic and familiar game.

GROUP SIZE: SMALL GROUPS • WHOLE GROUP

MATERIALS a jump rope of any size

FIRST, after students have been introduced to every lowercase cursive letter, invite them to play a cursive jump-rope game. One student jumps while chanting the alphabet in order. The rest of the group observes.

NEXT, when a student misses a jump, he or she arranges the jump rope on the ground to form the letter on which the jump was missed.

LAST, the rest of the group checks the formation of the letter and, if necessary, gives feedback on how to make it more readable. For a fun twist, challenge students to form short words with their rope!

ESL/ELD Connection Students unfamiliar with the English alphabet will hear it over and over.

38 Walk It!

Students walk through letter pathways.

GROUP SIZE: SMALL GROUPS

MATERIALS several large, thick pieces of sidewalk chalk

FIRST, write several letters in cursive on an outdoor surface—perhaps the playground surface—in chalk. Make them at least five feet tall.

NEXT, invite one child to stand on the starting point of one of the letters.

LAST, read the letter story (found on the Letter Practice pages, 28–47) aloud and ask the student to walk in time to your rhyming directions. Speed up for a challenge!

ESL/ELD Connection This activity is based on the Total Physical Response (TPR) method developed by James Asher, which uses movement as a bridge to language learning. Children experience and internalize language, following physical commands before being asked to produce speech.

39 Blind Writing

Students use visual and physical memory together to form letters and words.

GROUP SIZE: INDIVIDUAL

MATERIALS pencils and blank paper for each student

FIRST, choose several letters for students to practice. Write the letters on the board or have students look at models at their desks, perhaps from their letter practice card collection.

NEXT, have students put their pencils on blank sheets of paper at the starting point of the letter. They should then close their eyes and try to write the letter several times, then open their eyes and look at their work.

LAST, help students self-assess. How was their "blind" writing different from their "sighted" writing?

40 Ghost Writing

Students "feel" the movement associated with the formation of each letter, then self-check by "revealing" the letter.

GROUP SIZE: INDIVIDUALS OR PARTNERS

MATERIALS lemon or grapefruit juice, milk, Q-tips, a lamp or iron, blank white paper (you can also use commercially available invisible ink markers from toy and stationery stores)

FIRST, discuss uses of invisible ink with the group (many students will associate it with spying). Explain that our hands and brains know how to write, even if we can't see what we're writing, and that invisible ink can help prove it.

NEXT, invite students to dip their Q-tips into the lemon juice, grapefruit juice, or milk and write messages on their blank paper. Let them dry.

LAST, students can hold up their "invisible" message to a lightbulb, lightly rub against the bulb, and watch it appear! (Students should be closely supervised as they rub their messages against the bulbs.) For faster results, you can sandwich students' papers between a folded paper grocery bag and rub with a medium-hot iron. If students are working in partners, one may write and the other may read the result. Watch messages appear!

Auditory Learners

Auditory learners need to hear information because they remember best what they hear and say. They benefit from memory tricks such as rhyme and repeating what they hear. Sound-symbol associations play a large role in their learning, as do describing and discussing letter forms, hearing "stories" about how to form each letter, and taking oral directions as they write.

41 Who Am I?

Students use oral cues to form a mental image of letter shapes.

GROUP SIZE: WHOLE GROUP

MATERIALS none

FIRST, choose a letter to describe.

NEXT, ask students to close their eyes and imagine the letter you are describing. For instance, you might say: *I'm a "mountain climber." Start at the bottom line. Go up a very steep hill, slide straight down, go up into a little tummy, tuck it in, slide down again. Who am I?* Speak slowly so that students can visualize the letter. If not everyone has figured it out, give another clue, such as, *I'm so tall I can fly my own kite.*

LAST, invite students to call out the letter you described: k!

Teacher Tip

"When referring to the tall letters, I tell students that they are 'bumping their heads' on the top line. This reminds them to make their letters tall enough."

—*Ruby Schrimmer, Kathleen E. Goodwin School, Old Saybrook, Connecticut*

42 Cursive Construction Company

Students follow verbal instructions to "build" a letter.

GROUP SIZE: PARTNERS

MATERIALS pencil and paper for each student

FIRST, have partners decide who will be the site supervisor and who will be the builder. Using their own words, the site supervisor should describe the letter to the builder, step by step. He or she should speak slowly enough so that partners have time to write as they receive instructions.

NEXT, the site supervisor ends by saying something like, "You should have just built a *k*."

LAST, have partners switch roles and build another letter.

ESL/ELD Connection
Children will develop their ability to give and take directions in English.

43 Tongue Twisters

Students write their own alliterative tongue twisters.

GROUP SIZE: INDIVIDUALS • PARTNERS

MATERIALS pencil and paper for each student

FIRST, ask students to choose one letter with which to make a tongue twister. They might choose the first letter of their name or a letter they have recently learned.

NEXT, have them write out their creations in cursive, such as:

Silly Sammy spins and slips on a spilled smoothie.

LAST, have them write the tongue twister on the board so the group can try it!

44 The Name Game

Students associate initial sounds with capital cursive forms while sharpening their alphabetizing skills.

GROUP SIZE: PARTNERS

MATERIALS cut-out letter cards

FIRST, have partners lay out all their capital letter cards faceup on the floor, not in alphabetical order.

NEXT, say the first and last names of each child in the class one at a time, emphasizing the initial sounds. As you do so, students should pick out the correct initial letters for each first and last name. They should then place the letter cards alphabetically in a row.

LAST, challenge students to make up names that include letters not yet called ("Priscilla" and "X-Ray" for *P* and *X*, for example). You might start with "Ramona Quimby" to include *Q*, if there are no *Q*'s in the group. Students should end up with an alphabetized row of capital letters. Speed up the game for a challenge!

ER
art
ankle

Handwriting Hospital

Once students have completed the letter practice section and experienced lots of the activities, you might ask them to begin to write in cursive in their daily work. Many students who form letters perfectly on the letter practice pages will still need fine-tuning as they begin to use cursive for their everyday writing needs. They might become less aware of their handwriting. This is natural; their focus will be more on what they are writing and less on the perfect formation of letters!

Handwriting Hospital will help students specifically and carefully assess their own handwriting, and it will give you an organized system to help them do so. Teachers differ on the question of whether to grade handwriting; it's helpful to remember that legibility is the goal and that as students grow, they will develop a style that rarely looks exactly like the perfect models presented in the letter practice pages.

Cursive Doctor

Copy pages 75 and 76 for students. Let them "diagnose" the letters and "treat" them! This will pave the way for more specific self-assessment and "treatment" in one or more of the five hospital rooms.

Handwriting Hospital: The Five Rooms

Help students focus on specific problems in their handwriting. When you observe problems in the written work they turn in, choose from the five pages (pages 77–81) to identify problems. Since many students view the rewriting of an entire assignment as a punishment, and such a task can prove frustrating for students who struggle with fine-motor tasks, simply circle (or have students circle) the five words in their assignment that would be the most difficult for someone else to read. Hand their work back to them with the appropriate sheet. (You might also keep stacks of these sheets in a corner labeled "Handwriting Hospital," asking students to take their work to that corner and choose the appropriate sheet to work on.)

Key to Legibility

Reproduce "The Five S's of Cursive" on page 74 and laminate it for students who are having difficulty writing legibly. Review it with students, then ask them to use a wipe-off marker to check their work before turning it in. They might even tape it to their desks.

Name ______________________________

a b c d e f g h i j k l m n o p q r s t u v w x y z

The Five S's of Cursive

Make sure everyone can read what you've written!
Check off each "S" after you examine your writing.
Check your letters against a model.

☐ 

Are my letters too tall or short?
Do they sit neatly on the line?

☐ Shape

Are my letters closed up where they should be?
Are they too thin or too wide?

☐ 

Are my letters all slanting in the same direction?

☐ 

Are the spaces between my letters and words even?

☐ 

Did I press down evenly on the paper?
Is my writing light in places and heavy in others?
Is it too heavy or too light?

Name ____________________

a b c d e f g h i j k l m n o p q r s t u v w x y z

Be a Cursive Doctor!
Say what's wrong with these sick words and letters.
Then help them get better.

Size Healthy letters are the right height and rest neatly on the "ground" or bottom line. Which of these is easiest to read?

doctor doctor doctor

Shape Healthy letters are "closed up" where they should be, and are not too thin or wide. Which of these is easiest to read?

hospital hospital hospital

Slant Healthy letters slant in the same direction. If letters point straight up, forward, or lean backward a little, that's fine. They shouldn't point in different directions, though! Which of these is easiest to read?

sick sick sick

Word	What's Wrong?	Make It Better!
pencil	☐ Size ☐ Shape ☐ Slant	
pen	☐ Size ☐ Shape ☐ Slant	
pencil	☐ Size ☐ Shape ☐ Slant	
cursive	☐ Size ☐ Shape ☐ Slant	

a b c d e f g h i j k l m n o p q r s t u v w x y z

Be a Cursive Doctor!
Say what's wrong with these sick words and letters.
Then help them get better.

Spacing Healthy words are made up of letters that are evenly spaced. Which of these is easiest to read?

cursive cursive cursive

Smoothness Healthy letters have an "even line." If the line is too heavy or too light (or both heavy and light in the same word!), it's harder to read. Which of these is easiest to read?

heavy light uneven smooth

Word	What's Wrong?	Make It Better!
sick	☐ Spacing ☐ Smoothness	
healthy	☐ Spacing ☐ Smoothness	
The	☐ Spacing ☐ Smoothness	
doctor	☐ Spacing ☐ Smoothness	
hospital	☐ Spacing ☐ Smoothness	

a b c d e f g h i j k l m n o p q r s t u v w x y z

The Size Room

Emergency!

These letters and words have "size sickness." Circle the healthy one.

size Size size

Now, circle up to five "patients" for the Size Room on your paper (your teacher can help you). Then treat them! Write the words or sentences that are hard to read on the following lines.

Hint: Are you looking at the middle line? It's like the dotted line on a highway—drivers don't cross it before they think!

1

2

3

4

5

a b c d e f g h i j k l m n o p q r s t u v w x y z

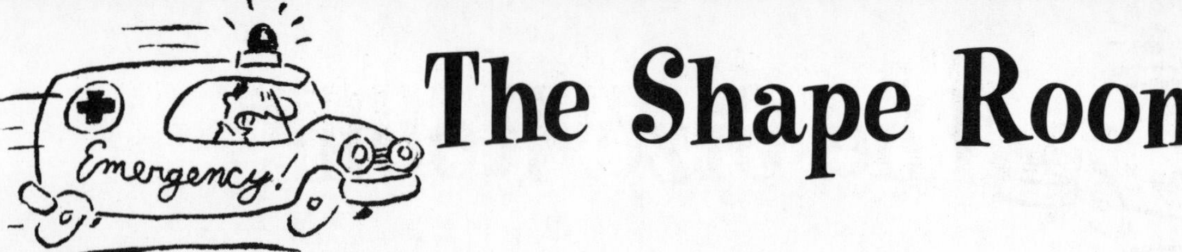

The Shape Room

These letters and words have "shape sickness." Circle the healthy one.

shape shape shape

Circle up to five "patients" for the Shape Room on your paper (your teacher can help you). Then treat them! Write the words or sentences that are hard to read on the following lines.

> **Hint:** Look at your model whenever you're not sure where letters close up.

1 ____________________

2 ____________________

3 ____________________

4 ____________________

5 ____________________

Name ____________________

a b c d e f g h i j k l m n o p q r s t u v w x y z

The Slant Room

These letters and words have "slant sickness." Circle the healthy one.

Circle up to five "patients" for the Slant Room in the on your paper (your teacher can help you). Then treat them! Write the words or sentences that are hard to read on the following lines.

Hint: Is your paper in the correct position?

1

2

3

4

5

Try This! Hold a deck of cards straight up on a tabletop. Make them slant one way, them the other, then straight up. Now try to make different cards slant different ways. Which is easier?

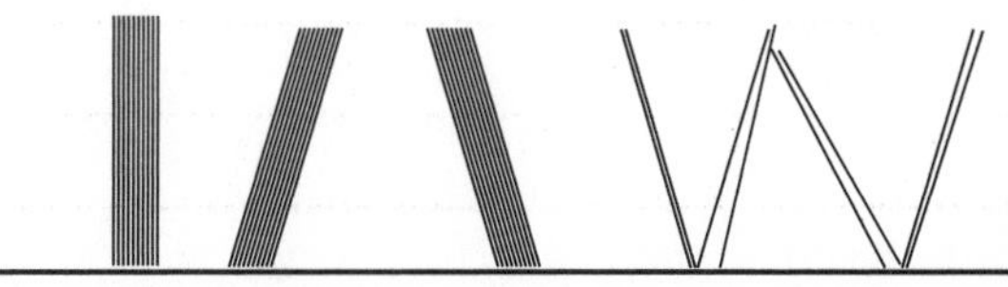

a b c d e f g h i j k l m n o p q r s t u v w x y z

The Spacing Room

These letters and words have "spacing sickness." Circle the healthy one.

space s pace space

Circle up to five "patients" for the Space Room on your paper (your teacher can help you). Then treat them! Write the words or sentences that are hard to read on the following lines.

> **Hint:** Make a "cursive ruler"! Take a small popsicle stick and use it to measure the space between each word in your sentence. You can also use your finger!

1 ____

2 ____

3 ____

4 ____

5 ____

Name ______________________________

a b c d e f g h i j k l m n o p q r s t u v w x y z

The Smoothness Room

These letters and words have "smoothness sickness." Circle the healthy one.

smooth smooth smooth

Circle up to five "patients" for the Smoothness Room on your paper (your teacher can help you). Then treat them! Write the words or sentences that are hard to read on the following lines.

Hint: Turn your paper over. Can you feel little ridges from the pencil pushing through? If you can, you're probably pressing down too hard. Are your letters too wobbly? Hold your pencil tighter.

1 ______________________________

2 ______________________________

3 ______________________________

4 ______________________________

5 ______________________________

Try This! To make sure you're holding the pencil correctly, wrap a rubber band around the pencil, an inch from the point. Hold your pencil above the rubber band.

a b c d e f g h i j k l m n o p q r s t u v w x y z

Additional Reproducibles

a b c d e f g h i j k l m n o p q r s t u v w x y z

Name ____________________

a b c d e f g h i j k l m n o p q r s t u v w x y z

Sign Up!

Signatures are one way people show they agree with something that is written. Most people have a special way of signing their name. See if you can match the famous person to his or her signature.

Walt Disney, the creator of Disneyland

Babe Ruth, the great baseball player

Susan B. Anthony, a leader for women's right to vote

Thomas Edison, the inventor of the lightbulb

George Washington, the first U.S. president

Francis Scott Key, the writer of the "Star-Spangled Banner"

L. Frank Baum, the writer of *The Wizard of Oz*

Martin Luther King, Jr., the civil rights leader

G Washington

F S Key

Thomas A Edison

Walt Disney

Martin Luther King Jr

L Frank Baum

Babe Ruth

Susan B. Anthony

Do you already know how to sign your name in cursive? Sign your name here any way you like. Notice how the people above "played" with their signatures. Try signing a few different ways and circle your favorite.

Name ______________________________

a b c d e f g h i j k l m n o p q r s t u v w x y z

Loopy Letters

Some letters have loops that point up.
Color in the loops.

b e h k l bike bike

bear bear like like

bake bake hello hello

Some letters have loops that point down.
Color in the loops.

g j p q y z pay pay

jeep jeep gap gap

quiz quiz jump jump

Only one does both!
Color in the loops.

f forget forget if if

lift lift fish fish

Cursive Concentration

a	*a*	b	*b*	c
c	d	*d*	e	*e*
f	*f*	g	*g*	h
h	i	*i*	j	*j*
k	*k*	l	*l*	m

m

Cursive Concentration

z

n	n	o	o	p
p	q	q	r	r
s	s	t	t	u
u	v	v	w	w
x	x	y	y	z

Name ____________________

a b c d e f g h i j k l m n o p q r s t u v w x y z a b c d e f g h i j k

Read Me

Look at each row. Circle the word or words that are easiest to read.

slant slant slant slant slant

shape shape shape shape shape

size size size size size size

smoothness smoothness

smoothness smoothness

spacing spacing spacing

spacing spacing

Name ____

a b c d e f g h i j k l m n o p q r s t u v w x y z

Letter Match

Match the cursive letters to their partners.

j	a	q	n
m	b	w	o
c	c	o	p
a	d	z	q
h	e	v	r
k	f	p	s
e	g	y	t
d	h	s	u
f	i	u	v
b	j	n	w
i	k	t	x
l	l	r	y
g	m	x	z

Name ______________________________

a b c d e f g h i j k l m n o p q r s t u v w x y z

Letter Match

Match the cursive letters to their partners.

F	A	R	N
J	B	Z	O
B	C	V	P
L	D	P	Q
A	E	N	R
H	F	S	S
E	G	Q	T
K	H	Y	U
D	I	X	V
M	J	W	W
I	K	U	X
G	L	O	Y
C	M	T	Z

Name

a b c d e f g h i j k l m n o p q r s t u v w x y z

Height Chart

Short

Medium

Tall

Underwater

Name ____________________

a b c d e f g h i j k l m n o p q r s t u v w x y z

Height Chart

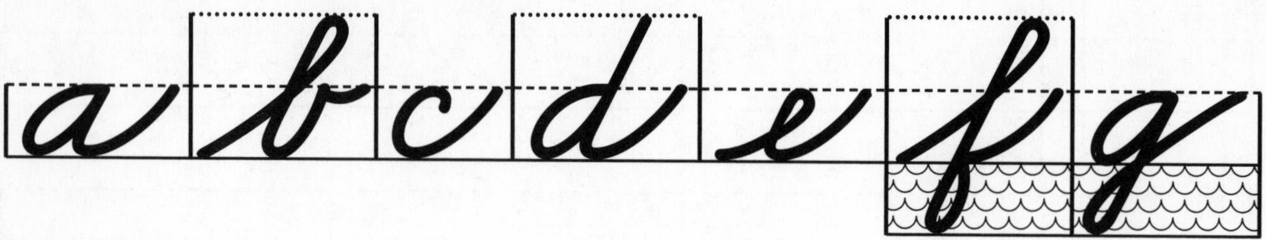

h i j k l m

n o p q r s t

u v w x y z

Cursive Calendar

Certificate of Completion

Congratulations!

You took the Cursive Challenge!

WRITE YOUR NAME IN PEN HERE: ________________________

WRITE THE NAME OF YOUR SCHOOL HERE: ________________________

____

TEACHER'S SIGNATURE

____

STUDENT'S SIGNATURE

Cursive Chit-Chat

FOLD HERE

From: ____________________

To: ____________________

____

____

____

FOLD HERE

Name ____________________

Lowercase Letters

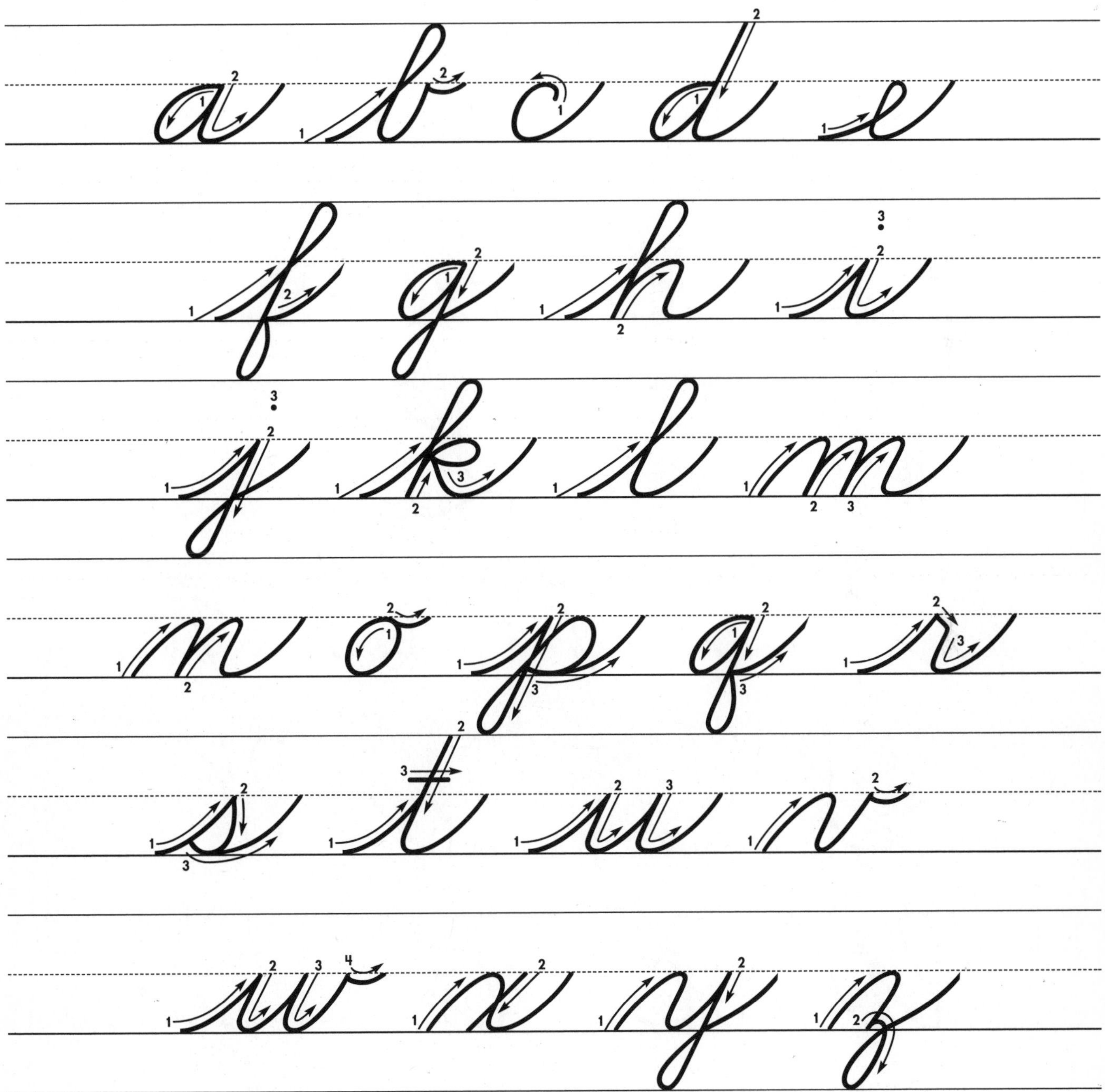

Name

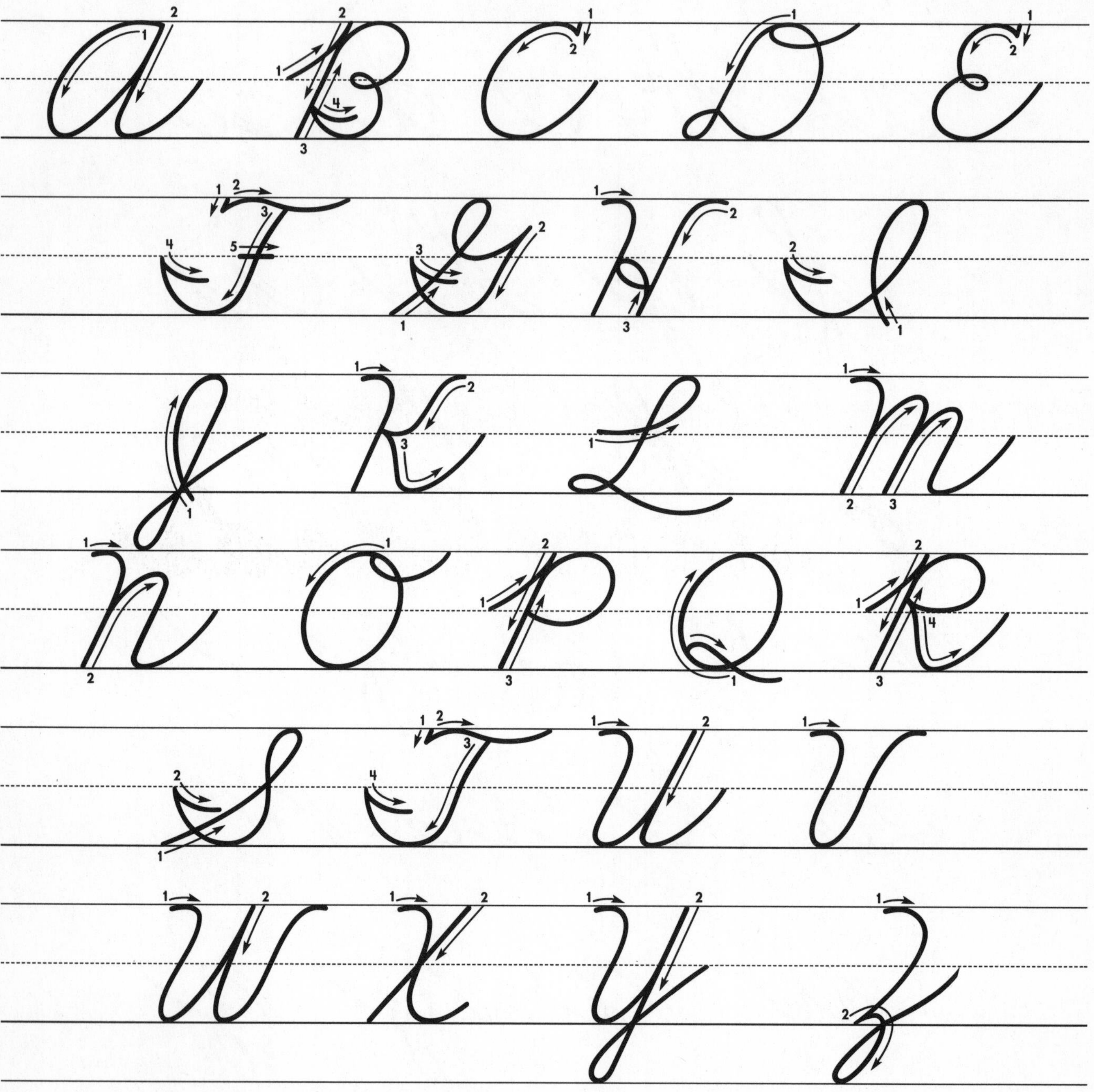

Uppercase Letters

a b c d e f g h i j k l m n o p q r s t u v w x y z

My Best Letter Cards

a b c d e f g h i j k l m n o p q r s t u v w x y z

My Best Letter Cards

My Best *i*

My Best *t*

My Best *u*

My Best *w*

My Best *e*

My Best Letter Cards

My Best *l*

My Best *b*

My Best *h*

My Best *k*

My Best *r*

My Best *s*

My Best *f*

My Best *p*

My Best *j*

My Best Letter Cards

My Best *a*

My Best *d*

My Best *g*

My Best *q*

My Best *o*

My Best *c*

My Best Letter Cards

My Best *n*

My Best *m*

My Best *v*

My Best *x*

My Best *y*

My Best *z*

My Best Letter Cards

My Best A

My Best O

My Best D

My Best C

My Best E

My Best Q

My Best Letter Cards

My Best *l*

My Best *f*

My Best Letter Cards

My Best *N*

My Best *M*

My Best *W*

My Best *H*

My Best *K*

My Best *X*

My Best *U*

My Best *Y*

My Best *V*

My Best *Z*

My Best Letter Cards

My Best *P*

My Best *R*

My Best *B*

My Best Letter Cards

My Best *T*

My Best *F*

My Best Letter Cards

My Best *G*

My Best *S*

My Best *L*

Bibliography

Many of the activities in this book reflect the ideas developed in the following books:

Adams, Marilyn Jager. 1990. *Beginning to Read: Thinking and Learning About Print.* Cambridge: The MIT Press.

Arena, John I., ed. 1970. *Building Handwriting Skills in Dyslexic Children.* San Rafael, CA: Academic Therapy Publications. (Banas, Norma, and I. J. Wills, "The Vulnerable Child and Cursive Writing." King, Diana Hanbury, "Some Practical Considerations in the Teaching of Handwriting." Larson, Charlotte E., "Teaching Beginning Writing." Ramming, Jessie, "Using the Chalkboard to Overcome Handwriting Difficulties.")

Asher, James. 1996. *Learning Another Language Through Actions.* Los Gatos, CA: Sky Oaks Productions.

Bear, D. R., S. Templeton, M. Invernizzi, and F. Johnston. 1996. *Words Their Way: Word Study for Phonics, Vocabulary and Spelling Instruction.* Englewood Cliffs, NJ: Merrill/Prentice Hall.

Blevins, Wiley. 1998. *Phonics A–Z: A Practical Guide.* New York: Scholastic.

Block, Cathy Collins. 1993. *Teaching the Language Arts.* Boston: Allyn & Bacon.

Eich, Joan. 1993. "Capitalizing on Modality Strengths: In D'Nealian Handwriting," Glenview, IL: ScottForesman.

Hamilton, Charles. 1979. *The Signature of America: A Fresh Look at Famous Handwriting.* New York: Harper & Row.

Kuhl, D., and P. Dewitz. 1994. "The Effect of Handwriting Style on Alphabet Recognition." Paper presented at the annual meeting of the American Education Research Association, New Orleans, LA.

Ruddell, Robert B., and Martha Rapp Ruddell. 1995. *Teaching Children to Read and Write: Becoming an Influential Teacher.* Boston: Allyn & Bacon.

Smith, Lyman D. 1892. *How to Teach Writing: A Manual of Penmanship Designed to Accompany Appleton's Standard Copy-Books.* New York: American Book Company.

Williams, Lena. 1995. "Can You Read This?" *The New York Times*, January 25.